Ancient People.

THE LOW COUNTRIES

General Editor

DR GLYN DANIEL

KING ALFRED'S COLLEGE
WINCHESTER

—

To be returned on or before the day marked
below:—

2 7 JAN 2003

PLEASE ENTER ON ISSUE SLIP:

AUTHOR DE LAET

TITLE L

ACCESSION N

DR GLYN DANIEL *Ancient Peoples and Places*

THE LOW COUNTRIES

S. J. De Laet

63 PHOTOGRAPHS

32 LINE DRAWINGS

A TABLE AND A MAP

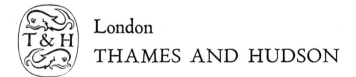

London

THAMES AND HUDSON

© THAMES AND HUDSON LONDON 1958
PRINTED IN GREAT BRITAIN
BY WESTERN PRINTING SERVICES
BRISTOL

THIS IS VOLUME FIVE IN THE SERIES
ANCIENT PEOPLES AND PLACES

To L.S.L.

CONTENTS

ILLUSTRATIONS

Acknowledgements

It is my pleasant duty to thank all those who have helped me in writing this book. For illustrations kindly placed at my disposal, I am most grateful to my colleagues H. Brunsting (Leyden), P. Coremans (Brussels), Count J. de Borchgrave d'Altena (Brussels), Mrs G. Faider-Feytmans (Mariemont), W. Glasbergen (Amsterdam), P. Moison (Mons), J. Philippe (Liège), F. Twiesselmann (Brussels), A. E. van Giffen (Groningen), and H. T. Waterbolk (Groningen). My colleagues and friends W. Glasbergen (Amsterdam), J. D. van der Waals (Amsterdam), and Mrs L. Kaelas (Stockholm) have very kindly allowed me to read and use in manuscript important monographs, which at the time of writing were still unpublished, and to them I am especially indebted. W. Glasbergen, Mrs L. Kaelas, F. Twiesselmann and I. Scollar have read the whole or part of the text before publication and pointed out several inaccuracies, which were subsequently corrected; they have my deepest gratitude. Lastly, my assistant, J. A. E. Nenquin, has undertaken the thankless task of translating my text into English. He too deserves a share of my thanks. Finally, I wish to thank my colleague Glyn Daniel, editor of the 'Ancient Peoples and Places' series, for his valuable help and advice.

31.12.56   S. J. D. L.

Introduction

WHEN I WAS ASKED by my colleague Glyn E. Daniel to write a book on the prehistory of the Low Countries for the 'Ancient Peoples and Places' series, which he directs with his well-known competence and energy, I accepted his offer somewhat light-heartedly. It was only after having drawn the first general sketch of the work that I realized how difficult it was going to be to condense into something like 40,000 words the ancient history of the area under consideration, from the first appearance of man onwards to the Roman Conquest, near the very beginning of our era.

This object has not been easy to achieve. Indeed, to describe the prehistory of Belgium and the Netherlands, and to give it the place it deserves in the general European picture, means nothing less than considering the prehistory of all Western and Northern Europe. Practically, all cultural tendencies and all civilizations which characterized this part of the world in pre-historic times can be found—sometimes very attenuated, it is true—in our regions. This results more from the geographical position of the Low Countries than from their physical aspect or their natural wealth. The whole area—except the fertile zone in central Belgium and Dutch Limburg—was indeed at that period not very attractive from a settler's point of view: the rather sterile Ardennes highlands, covered with dense forests, the sandy soils and the marshy lowlands continually threatened by disastrous floods, formed the bulk of the territory. The subsoil, too, was rather poor, at least in products which might have at-tracted prehistoric man. The exploitation of flint deposits alone gave rise to a certain amount of trade during neolithic times. But here no copper, no tin, no silver, no amber are to be found. It is only at the end of the protohistoric period that iron began to be industrially worked, while coal-mining comes much later still, during the Middle Ages. If the Low Countries are, at the present day, areas of intensive agriculture and very specialized industry—thus having become at the same time one of the gardens of Europe as well as extremely active industrial centres and, in consequence, having the world's densest population—this is due to the increasing activity of their inhabitants since the Middle Ages. In prehistoric times, nothing whatever pointed to such a development.

However, that so many successive cultures are to be found here, notwithstanding this poverty and inhospitable nature, is due above all to the geographical situation of our regions. The Low Countries form the western extremity of the great Baltic plain, where so many migrations and cultural movements coming from the north and the east faded out. It extends on both sides of the delta of three of the most important rivers of Western Europe, the Rhine, the Meuse and the Scheldt, which sometimes served as connecting links, sometimes as cultural barriers. The old primary formations of the Eifel and the Ardennes, relatively low and very much eroded, were but a negligible obstacle and have never prevented penetrations from the Rhineland or from Central Europe. The valleys of the Moselle and of the Meuse allowed an easy access to the south. More to the west, no natural barrier exists between central and lowland Belgium and northern France. Last of all, communications with the British Isles were no more difficult. During the whole of the Palaeolithic Period and part of the Mesolithic, a land-bridge existed between that country and the Continent, so that on both sides of the Channel similar or closely related cultures are to be found. But even after the sea had separated one from the other, maritime relations between Great Britain and our coastal plain remained easy, and numerous contacts, cultural movements, even migrations—from east to west, or from west to east—have strengthened relations between the two countries.

For these reasons, the Low Countries have from the very beginning formed a natural crossroad, a turn-table between East and West, North and South Europe. Thanks to the passing and the intersecting of the main roads followed by men and ideas, migrations and invasions, the Low Countries, notwithstanding their relatively small area, formed already in prehistoric times a sort of synthesis of Europe, just as is the case now.

Today, enclosed by France, Great Britain and Germany, all three nations of great political, economic and cultural importance, Belgium, the Netherlands and the Grand Duchy of Luxembourg present an undeniable unity, much stronger than the superficial economic and customs arrangement known as Benelux. This unity is much more apparent to foreigners than to the inhabitants of these countries themselves. These are much more conscious of the profound differences which separate them in many important points of culture, tradition, language, religion, economics. Our countries are not only divided by political frontiers, but also by the linguistic frontier (which runs through Belgium) between Romance and Germanic languages, and by the religious frontier (which runs through the Netherlands) between Roman Catholic and Protestant traditions. Inside our communities there thus exists a very unstable and fluid equilibrium between centripetal and centrifugal forces, which, now broken, then re-established again, has resulted in successive periods of political and cultural unity or violent opposition. The origins of this state of affairs, the reasons which explain these antitheses and these unitary trends, must be sought in remote times, and quite a few of them probably date already from the prehistoric period. The effects of this swing from collaboration between North and South to violent opposition and back again are felt to this day.

B.C.				HIGHLAND BELGIUM & LUXEMBURG (NAMUR, LUXEMBURG, Gr. DUCHY)	CENTRAL BELGIUM (HAINAUT, BELG. BRABANT, LIÈGE)	WESTERN B (EAST & WES⸳
0	SUBATLANTIC	END OF PRE-HISTORIC PERIOD	IRON AGE	ROMAN CONQUEST		
200				HUNSRÜCK-EIFEL CIVILIZATION	LATÈNE GROUP OF HAINAUT	NORTHER⸳
400		HALSTATT CIVIL-IZATION & BEGIN-NINGS OF IRON AGE		HALLSTATT WARRIORS		
600					PROTO-CELTIC	URNFI⸳
800						
1000	SUBBOREAL	BRONZE AGE	BRONZE AGE			D R⸳
1200						
1400						H I L⸳
1600		LATE NEOLITHIC MIGRATIONS				B E⸳
1800				S O M CIVILIZATION		
2000						
2200						
2400	ATLANTIC	DIFFUSION OF NEOLITHIC WAY OF LIFE	NEOLITHIC			
2600				MICHELSBERG CIVILIZATION +		
2800				SECONDARY NEOLITHIC CIVILIZATION⸳		
3000				PRE-CAMPIGNIAN		
3500		FIRST AGRICULTURAL COMMUNITIES				
4000				UPPER TARDENOISIAN	DANUBIAN	UPPER T⸳
5000	BOREAL	MESOLITHIC FOOD-GATHERERS	MESOLITHIC	TARDENOISIAN		MAGLE⸳
6000						
7000	PREBOREAL					
8000	YOUNGER DRYAS			EPIMAGDALENIAN		
9000	ALLERØD OSCILLATION					
10000		UPPER PALAEOLITHIC REINDEER HUNTERS				
11000	OLDER DRYAS		PALAEOLITHIC	MAGDALENIAN		
12000				AURIGNACIAN		
	LATE WÜRM	THE FIRST INHABITANTS				
	EARLY WÜRM			MOUSTERIAN		
	RISS-WÜRM INTERGLACIAL			LEVALLOISO-MOUSTERIAN		
	?			MESVINIAN		
	?			ACHEULEAN		
	?			CLACTONIAN		

Fig. 1. Tab⸳

16

NORTH BELGIUM & SOUTH NETHERLANDS (BELG. & DUTCH LIMBURG, ANTWERP & N. BRABANT)	WESTERN NETHERLANDS (ZEELAND, N.&S. HOLLAND, UTRECHT)	EASTERN NETHERLANDS (DRENTHE, OVERIJSSEL, GUELDERS)	NORTHERN NETHERLANDS (FRISIA, GRONINGEN)	B.C.
	R O M A N	C O N Q U E S T		0
NE GROUP		URNFIELDS	EARLY TERPEN CIVILIZATION	200
				400
IELDS		URNFIELDS		600
IGRATION		PROTO-GERMANIC URNFIELD IMMIGRATION		800
N S T E I N U R N S		D R A K E N S T E I N U R N S		1000
				1200
S U M U R N S		H I L V E R S U M U R N S		1400
				1600
E R C I V I L I Z A T I O N S				1800
				2000
				2200
		FUNNEL BEAKER CIVILIZATION		2400
		+		2600
	S E C O N D A R Y N E O L I T H I C C I V I L I Z A T I O N S			2800
				3000
OISIAN DANUBIAN	UPPER TARDENOISIAN		OLDESLOE	3500
				4000
N T A R D E N O I S I A N	M A G L E M O S E A N		T A R D E N O I S I A N	5000
				6000
				7000
				8000
AHRENSBURG				9000
TJONGER GROUP		T J O N G E R G R O U P		10000
				11000
	H A M B U R G I A N			12000

ds and cultures.

Fig. 2. Map of the Low Countries, showing the provinces and the main natural regions.

CHAPTER I

The First Inhabitants

D URING PLEISTOCENE TIMES, considerable geological and climatic differences existed between Belgium and
the Netherlands. Because of these, human occupation was far
from being the same in both regions during the earliest prehistoric periods. These differences also had their influence on the
state of conservation of the occupational remains.

Since the beginning of the Quaternary Period, Belgium has
formed part of the Continent and has never again been covered
by the sea, with the occasional exception of a narrow coastal
strip, parallel with the present-day shore-line; the ice-cap itself
has never reached it. On the other hand, the periglacial climate
that existed during glacial times and the important climatic
variations strongly influenced the morphology of the land (formation of river-terraces, deposits by snow and wind, niveo-
fluvial deposits, solifluxion, etc.). All these changes were much
more important in the Netherlands. Several times in fact this
region has, wholly or partially, been covered by the sea in
quaternary times. On top of this, the most southerly limit of the
ice during the Riss glaciation followed a line going from
NW to SE, from Vogelenzang (near Haarlem), Utrecht,
Rhenen, to Nijmegen. All such disturbances had a profound
influence on the morphology of these regions.

From this it will be apparent that the oldest human remains
found *in situ* in undisturbed geological layers belong, in Belgium, to the last phase of the third glaciation or even to the last
interglacial (end of the Lower Palaeolithic), and in the Netherlands to the final phase of the last glaciation (final Upper
Palaeolithic). It is nevertheless certain that man has occupied
this region—or at least part of it—at a much earlier date,
although the oldest human industries discovered are much more

recent than the ones found in northern France and England. No equipment of the Cromer or Ipswich industries, nor of the Abbevillian has up to now been found in the Low Countries.[1]

The most ancient industry discovered in Belgium is the Clactonian. It is identical with the classic Clactonian from England

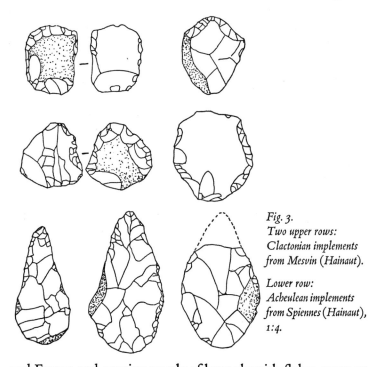

Fig. 3.
Two upper rows:
Clactonian implements
from Mesvin (Hainaut).

Lower row:
Acheulean implements
from Spiennes (Hainaut),
1:4.

and France and consists mostly of large shortish flakes, more or less ovoid in shape, the sides crudely retouched or adapted for prehension; there are also concave scrapers, natural flakes shaped by side-retouching, and nuclei adapted by regularization of the edges. These Clactonian implements, made from brown flint and all very much rolled, were found in much eroded and soliflucted gravels at Spiennes and Mesvin during the construction of the Mons-Binche railroad.

Fig. 3

These two sites (Spiennes and Mesvin) (Hainaut),[2] together with a few phosphated chalk works in the same region (Saint-Symphorien, Mesvin-Ciply, Elouges, Cuesmes, Baudour), have yielded an Acheulean industry, less rolled and—Breuil says—not so old as the Clactonian. Typologically some of these bifaces may be related to the older Acheulean, but most of them seem to belong to the middle Acheulean; however, since they have been discovered in soliflucted gravel and in a rolled condition, it is difficult to be definite about this.

Fig. 3

A few surface finds of Acheulean-type implements have been reported from Belgium and even a couple from the Netherlands.[3] Their number is much too small to allow us to determine whether they are traces of a continuous occupation of the Low Countries before the Riss ice advance, or only the relics of occasional incursions from hunters coming from the South or the East.

Let us reconsider the valley of the Haine, near Mons. An industry has been discovered here which seems to form a transition between the Clactonian and the Levalloiso-Mousterian. This rather rolled material—sometimes called 'Mesvinian'—is found in eroded and soliflucted gravels. The principal site is the Hélin quarry at Spiennes. It is a flake-industry announcing the Levallois technique. Most typical are the rather numerous blades, small flakes closely resembling Levallois objects, and sub-triangular flakes of medium size. These flakes have been made by irregular and crude trimming into hardly specialized implements used for scraping, cutting and piercing. Bifaces are completely missing.

Fig. 4

None of the three above-mentioned cultures has been found in an undisturbed layer. The same is not true however of the Levalloiso-Mousterian (or older Mousterian) which will now be described.[4]

This Levalloiso-Mousterian industry is characterized by the prepared platform of Levallois-type, Levallois and triangular

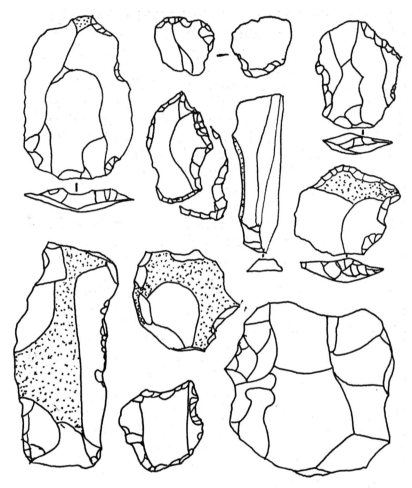

Fig. 4. Mesvinian implements from the Hélin quarry at Spiennes (Hainaut), 1:2.

flakes, scrapers, points, notched scrapers, knives and subtriangular, cordiform or lanceate bifaces. A few bifaces of final
Acheulean type (Micoque) are also found. It is well represented
in Belgium, mostly in the Haine valley at the sites already men-

Fig. 5

tioned (Spiennes and Mesvin railroad trench, Hélin quarry at Spiennes, Saint-Symphorien, Mesvin-Ciply, etc.). The industry seems to form a complete evolutionary series and is found *in situ* in several geological strata. Some of these strata (e.g. the sand-deposits of the Hélin quarry and at Saint-Symphorien) might go back as far as the last interglacial, while others (the base gravels of the younger loess at Spiennes, Mesvin, Hélin quarry) correspond with the beginning of the Würm glaciation. These later layers also contain specimens of a fauna characterized by mammoth and rhinoceros tichorinus.

The Levalloiso-Mousterian has been found in other places in Belgium, namely in Hainaut (Hainaut quarries and Clypot quarry at Soignies) and in the province of Liège (Sainte-Walburge). All these sites are in undetermined quaternary gravels and can teach us nothing about the dwellings of lower palaeolithic man. For this reason, one site is especially important: the cave of the Hermitage quarry, in the Méhaigne valley (prov. Liège), between Huccorgne and Moha, where a considerable number of artefacts of this period have been discovered. Therefore it may be thought that lower palaeolithic man already took refuge in caves, just like the people from middle and upper palaeolithic times. We know next to nothing of their mode of life, but it is self-evident that hunting—and perhaps fruit-picking—was their main source of food supply.

It might also be mentioned that a few surface finds of Levalloiso-Mousterian-type objects are known from the Netherlands, in the provinces of Limburg and North Brabant.

Finds from the Middle Palaeolithic are much more numerous and the sequence is much more complete than is the case for the previous period. The Mousterian is very well represented in Belgium, both in alluvial and in cave deposits; a certain number of surface finds and isolated objects are also known.

Most of the alluvial deposits are concentrated in the Haine valley (Spiennes and Mesvin trench, Hélin quarry, Stam- bruges, Mesvin-Ciply, Saint-Symphorien, Dethy sandpit near Bonsecours, etc.), around Soignies (Wincqz quarry, Hainaut quarries, Clypot quarry), near Liège (Sainte-Walburge), in Hesbaye (Kinart sandpit at Omal, Otrange, Huccorgne, etc.) and in Brabant (Bois de la Houssière, Ottembourg, Ottignies, Court-Saint-Etienne). The Mousterian industry is found there in layers (for instance the basal gravels and the oldest deposits of the younger loess) which are geologically dated to the first phases of the last glaciation. On the other hand, the caves in- habited by Mousterian man are mostly found in the Condroz region, in the valleys of the Meuse (caves at Engis, Hastière, etc.) and some of its tributaries and subsidiary rivers: the Méhaigne (cave 'du Docteur'), the Vesdre (caves at Fond-de- Forêt), the Lesse ('Trou de la Naulette' at Walzin), the Orneau (cave at Spy). A few isolated Mousterian or Mousteroid-type artefacts have been found in lowland Belgium (Flanders) and in the Netherlands (Limbourg and North Brabant), but again their number is too small and their date too uncertain to prove a continuous occupation during this period.

In contrast with the Lower Palaeolithic, a certain number of human fossils of middle palaeolithic age have been found in Belgium. The Neanderthal race, of which specimens have been found, *inter alia,* in Germany, France, Spain and Italy, in con- nection with Mousterian industry, is represented in Belgium at four different places. Two of these finds are of considerable his- toric interest, because they have allowed us for the first time to date Neanderthal man and to reconstruct his natural habitat. The Neanderthal skeleton, found in 1856, was without archaeological context. Nine years later, in 1865, E. Dupont discovered in the 'Trou de la Naulette' at Walzin, a jaw-bone, canine, cubitus and metatarsal of Neanderthal type; most significantly, these fossils, in excellent stratigraphical position,

were found together with important faunal remains representative of the period. In 1886, in a well characterized Mousterian
level, two almost complete Neanderthal skeletons were discovered by M. Lohest and M. De Puydt in the cave at Spy.
Part of a femur was found in the first cave at Fond-de-Forêt,

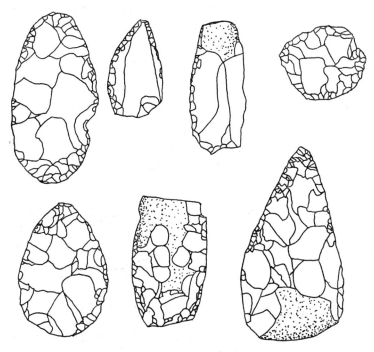

Fig. 5. *Levalloiso-Mousterian implements from Saint-Symphorien*
(Hainaut), 1:3.

and the skull of a child (perhaps dubious) in the second cave at
Engis. A description of Neanderthal man is out of place here; we
need only refer to any good book on prehistoric anthropology.

The Mousterian industry found in Belgium corresponds to
the artefacts found in Mousterian levels in Great Britain,
France, Germany, Switzerland, Spain, etc. This industry

lasted over a long period and it is possible to distinguish a certain typological evolution which, however, there is no need to go into here. It is a development of the Levalloiso-Mousterian, and is characterized by more and more specialized implements. Most typical of these are triangular or ogival points, and scrapers of different types, made from flakes trimmed along one side

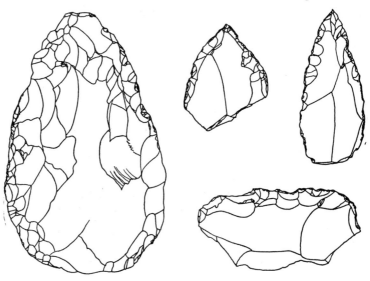

Fig. 6. Mousterian implements from the cave at Spy (prov. Namur), 1:2.

only. They are very well made, with long and regular retouches. Concave scrapers, knives, anvils, hammer stones and nuclei are found together with more archaic implements: cordiform and subtriangular bifaces and Levallois flakes. Together with the flint artefacts, worked bone appears: fragments of long bones, split for the extraction of the marrow, seem to have been used afterwards for retouching.

The cold and humid climate of the first Würm phases, although not so rigorous as during the Riss glaciation, forced man into the shelter of the caves. There we find the traces of

Fig. 6

his hearths, the remains of his equipment and of his meals. Big game was of paramount importance to his food supply. Mammoth, rhinoceros tichorinus, aurochs, horse, cervus ela/ phus, ibex, wolf and wild boar were extensively hunted. Reindeer too is found. All these animals were probably caught in traps and the carcasses divided on the spot. In general, only the larger parts of the skeleton are found inside the caves: hind/ quarters, legs and heads (these last for the extraction of the brain). The presence of coproliths of hyena and cave/bear in these caves, and whole skeletons of these animals in anatomical connection, suggest that they visited the caves during the absence of man to eat the remains of his meal. Occasionally, small game was caught (fox, wild dog, wild cat, marmot, squirrel, hare, weasel, wild duck, crow, thrush . . .), while fishing seems only to have played a lesser part (freshwater fish bones were found in the 'Trou de la Naulette').

It is not certain whether the Spy skeletons represent an inten/ tional burial, but finds from France indicate that Neanderthal man buried his dead with a certain amount of ceremonial: notwithstanding his still bestial looks, his mind was already aware of the mystery of death and the after/life.

CHAPTER II

The Upper Palaeolithic Reindeer-hunters

THE UPPER PALAEOLITHIC, belonging to the end phase of the Würm glaciation, can easily be distinguished from the previous periods. The climate in our regions was much more rigorous than it had been during the Riss glaciation, although the ice cap did not spread any further southwards than the mouth of the River Elbe. During the Aurignacian period, the climate, though cold, can still be described as being relatively temperate, only to become definitely Siberian during Magdalenian times, with very cold and dry winters and rather warm summers. Between the Scandinavian ice-sheet on one side, and the glaciers from the Alps on the other, a tundra zone existed in which the present hydrographic system took shape. The fauna too, had changed. While mammoth and rhinoceros tichorinus become more and more scarce, finally to disappear altogether, the inhabitants of our regions hunted animals then existing in large numbers, like reindeer, red deer, chamois, ibex, horse and bison. Other animals, too—brown bear, wolf, fox, arctic fox, badger, white grouse and lemming, typical of a periglacial climate—were extensively hunted.

Everywhere Neanderthal man had disappeared and his place been taken by *homo sapiens*, of whom several fossils, belonging to different races, have been found in adjacent countries. Upper palaeolithic fossils from our regions, however, are extremely rare.[1] Although in upper palaeolithic times the inhabitants of our region, like their predecessors from previous periods, still lived exclusively from the produce of the hunt—and in the first place from the reindeer-hunt, from the gathering of fruits and edible roots, and in ever-increasing manner from fishing, their mode of life had changed considerably in more than one aspect. Their equipment had become more specialized and diversified,

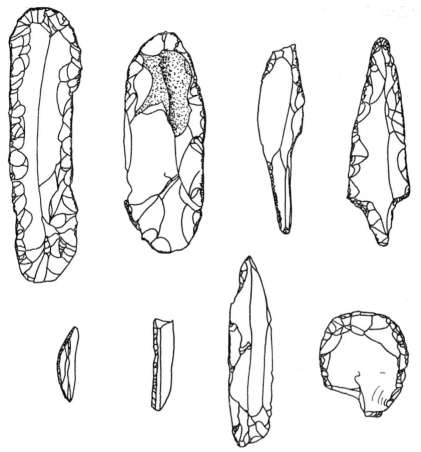

*Fig. 7. Aurignacian implements from the Trou-Magrite at Pont-à-Lesse
(prov. Namur), 3:4.*

their armament was much more perfect (throwing weapons, spears, spear-throwers, bows and arrows appeared). Not only flint, but bone, ivory, reindeer—and red deer—antlers were made use of. Lastly, one may conclude from a certain number of finds, that the mind of our ancestors began to be preoccupied with magic and religion on one side, with aesthetic considera- tions on the other; both seem to be closely related.

Another important change concerns more specially the Low Countries. While during the previous periods only some districts from central Belgium—in the provinces of Hainaut, Brabant, Namur and Liège—had been to a certain extent occupied, other regions were at present regularly visited by the reindeerhunters, namely the northern provinces of the Netherlands. One must bear in mind, however, that the upper palaeolithic cultures from Belgium represent the northwesternmost limit of the classic Aurignacian and Magdalenian as we know them from France, Spain, Switzerland and southern Germany; the implements found in the Netherlands, on the contrary, are closely related to the Hamburgian of northwestern Germany.

After a short description of the Belgian Aurignacian and Magdalenian,[2] we will say a few words about the Hamburgian from the Netherlands.

Apart from a few surface finds, the Aurignacian in Belgium is almost exclusively known from cave deposits[3] in the provinces of Namur ('Trou Magrite' at PontàLesse, caves at Goyet, Spy, PetitModave, MarchelesDames, Hastière, Montaigle, etc.) and Liège (cave 'du Docteur' near Huccorgne, caves of Engis, Martinrive, FonddeForêt, etc.). As a rule, the Aurignacian levels are stratigraphically welldefined, often under a Magdalenian layer, and contain hearths, foodremains, implements, arms and ornaments. Burials had not yet been discovered.

The flint industry is characterized by less massive artefacts, finely retouched and of a better finish than was the case during the previous period. Every implement is made to serve one welldefined purpose. Scrapers (corescrapers, nosescrapers, endscrapers, double scrapers), gravers (beaked gravers, double burins, etc.), blades (notched blades, pointed blades, *dos rabattu* blades), points (Font Robert tanged points, Gravette points) and awls are very numerous. We will not dwell upon the evolution of this industry; suffice it to say that while the Lower Aurignacian with its Châtelperron points is rather rare (Hastière, Engihoul, Montaigle), the Middle and Upper Aurignacian are very well represented.

Fig. 7

Fig. 8. Head and neck of an ibex, engraved on two sandstone tablets, from the third cave at Goyet (prov. Namur). Height 4¾ ins.

Bone, ivory and antler from reindeer and red deer were frequently made into implements and weapons. Amongst the most characteristic of these are the spear-heads: conical fragments of bone or antler, tapering to a sharp point, and mostly split at the base. The wooden shafts into which these points were fitted, have of course disappeared. Biconical points, pins, chisels, polishers, *retouchoirs* and a few *bâtons de commandement* are made from the same material.

Aurignacian man loved to adorn himself, as is proved by numerous finds of perforated animal teeth and shells, ivory beads, and bone, ivory or stone pendants. In the 'Trou Sandron', near Huccorgne, was found a complete necklace made from perforated wolf's teeth. Tattooing and body paint-ing seem to have been practised, probably with a magical pur-pose. Certain bone pins have been interpreted as tattooing instruments, and in quite a few caves haematite (oligiste) has been found—sometimes in large quantities, as at Spy, where one Aurignacian level was completely impregnated with it. This pigment was used for body painting or, as in certain adjacent regions where burials of this period have been discovered, to sprinkle over the dead body, again with magical intentions.

Cave art is entirely absent from the Low Countries, although a large number of Belgian caves are very suitable for painted or engraved decoration. On the other hand, we do possess a cer-tain number of objects proving that during the Aurignacian the inhabitants of our regions did share the magico-religious ideas of their more southerly neighbours. In the first place

Plate 1

comes the 'Venus' from the Trou-Magrite at Pont-à-Lesse: a mammoth-ivory figurine, $1\frac{5}{8}$ in. high, very clumsily made and which is probably only a rough sketch. Notwithstanding its primitive character, the statuette indubitably forms part of the series of Aurignacian 'Venuses', extending from Siberia to Western Europe. The same cave has yielded a fragment of reindeer antler, engraved with mysterious signs, which have been interpreted by some as fusiform fishes, by others as swans,

Plate 2

as ideograms or simply as decorative elements. In the Aurigna-cian level of the third cave at Goyet, some other interesting engraved objects have been discovered. Two reindeer-antler *bâtons de commandement*, of which the first, badly damaged, seems to be plain, the second being decorated with engraved

Plate 2

fishes (a trout, a pike and an undefined fish). The same level has yielded quite a few sandstone tablets, some of which are

engraved. Two fragments represent the head and neck of an
ibex; the head of a beast of prey amongst branches can be seen
on another piece, but this is not very well drawn.

Fig. 8

Certain archaeologists maintain that the Aurignacian in
Belgium can be divided into a classic Aurignacian and a
Périgordian; their arguments are not very convincing.

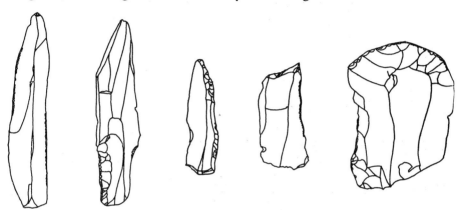

*Fig. 9. Magdalenian implements from the Trou du Frontal at Furfooz
(prov. Namur), 2:3.*

Like the Aurignacian, the Magdalenian in Belgium is only
known from cave deposits. The most important caves are in
the provinces of Namur (Châleux, Goyet, Trou du Frontal
and Trou des Nutons at Furfooz, Falaën) and Luxembourg
(Sy-Verlaine, cave 'du coléoptère' at Juzaine-Bomal).

The rather poor Magdalenian from Belgium is but a pale
reflection of its French counterpart. The lithic industry is
characterized by numerous *bec de flûte* gravers (already found in
the Upper Aurignacian), angle gravers, small notched blades,
dos rabattu blades, blade scrapers, awls. The *bec de perroquet*
gravers, so typical for the Magdalenian in France, are practically absent from Belgian deposits. Implements made from
bone and antler are even more perfect. Spear-heads, awls, eyed

Fig. 9

C

Fig. 10

*Fig. 10. Magdale-
nian harpoon with
double series of barbs,
from Goyet (prov.
Namur), about 1:2*

Plates 3, 4

needles are skilfully made. Harpoons with single or double
series of barbs are rather rare. The best specimen, made from
bone, was discovered at Goyet. It has a double series of barbs,
each barb having two parallel grooves, possibly to hold the
poison which the hunters used to smear on their throwing
weapons. Up to now, no spear-throwers have been found.

The liking for ornamentation, already much developed
during the Aurignacian age, remained. All the sites have
yielded pierced shells, some—fossilized and dating from the
Eocene—coming from the Champagne or even from the Paris
region. Perforated pebbles, bone and ivory pendants and perforated teeth are found. In the Goyet cave a complete necklace
of horse incisors has been discovered. In contrast with the
splendid revival of Magdalenian art in France and Spain, on
the Belgian sites only very few decorated objects have been
found, while parietal art is wholly absent. In the Trou du
Frontal at Furfooz, a series of sandstone (psammite) tablets
have been found, two of which, when put together, represent
the engraved hindpart of a walking *bos primigenius*. The excavation of the Trou de Châleux was more successful. A very vivid
representation of the head, antlers and neck of a deer is engraved on a schist tablet. On one side of a broken slab of sandstone, a *bos primigenius* and a deer are represented, superimposed;
a recumbent goat and several horses are sketched on the other
side. Lastly, the same deposit has yielded an ivory plaque
roughly fashioned to represent an animal silhouette. Two pendants may be mentioned; one from the cave at Juzaine-Bomal
represents a beetle, in ivory, with two holes bored through the
side of each wing-cover; the other one, found at Fond-de-Forêt
has the form of a fish. Two strange objects, whose authenticity
has sometimes been doubted, were discovered in the cave at
Sy-Verlaine. They are a pin with the head carved to represent
a bearded human face, and a pisciform ivory plaque, the eye of
the fish being used as a suspension hole.

To explain the poverty of the Belgian Magdalenian, the following, rather attractive hypothesis has been advanced: the climate being too cold, the reindeer-hunters did not stay continuously in Belgium. They followed their game during its seasonal migrations—like the modern Eskimo—visiting our regions in summertime, but spending the winter in central France, where the climate was less rigorous. This hypothesis might also explain the presence in the Belgian deposits, of the fossilized shells from Champagne and Seine-et-Oise. A similar reason has been given to explain the presence in the Netherlands of the Hamburgian reindeer-hunters, who will be discussed presently.

The presence of quantities of faked artefacts in certain collections has in the past made the study of the Dutch Palaeolithic rather difficult.[4] In fact, a few Acheulean, Levalloiso-Mousterian and Mousterian implements excepted, the oldest culture found in the Netherlands is the Hamburgian.

It is only about twenty years ago that this civilization was for the first time recognized. It was discovered near Hamburg, on the now famous site of Meiendorf and in the oldest Stellmoor level. A few years later a series of deposits of the same culture were found in the Netherlands, in the provinces of Frisia (Appelsga, Bakkeveen, Houtigehage, Makkinga, the best excavated site being at Ureterp), Groningen (Marum), Drenthe (Gasselte, Havelte, Rolde), Guelders (Elspeet, Harderwijk, Stroe) and Utrecht (Soest). In the sandy acid soil of these regions only the stone industry has been preserved, but in the peat-bogs of north-western Germany implements and weapons made from bone and antler were discovered.

During the last glaciation, the southern limit of the ice-cap did not descend as far as the mouth of the River Elbe. Large numbers of reindeer herds fed on the tundra vegetation of the vast plains extending between Schleswig-Holstein and England and as far as the Dogger Bank. In this region lived the Hamburgian hunters, following their game during its seasonal migrations. In summertime they put up their tents—probably made from reindeer-skins, traces of which have been found in Germany—near the edge of the ice-cap in Schleswig-Holstein, coming back to the south in the winter to their quarters in the northern part of the Netherlands.

Approximately speaking, the Hamburgian is contemporaneous with the Magdalenian, but several characteristics make a differentiation possible. Recent studies, based mainly on palynology, give a tentative date of 14,000 to 10,000 B.C. In fact, the origin of this culture must be sought in the Late Aurignacian from Bohemia, Poland and the Ukraine. The most typical stone artefacts are the shouldered or tanged points (often showing an oblique inverse retouch across the base), some of which seem to have been used as arrow-heads, while others, fixed in antler handles, were probably used for cutting. Typical, too, is the pseudo-awl on blades and flakes, with a bending point disposed at the middle or at one corner of one extremity of the flake, used to detach from the reindeer antlers long narrow strips which were made into harpoons, awls, needles and arrow-shafts. Different types of gravers, single and double blade scrapers, piercers, etc. are also found. A complete evolution can be established for this industry: the form of the tanged points changed, while the number of pseudo-awls diminished and the scrapers became more numerous.

Fig. 11

The German deposits also contain needles, awls and harpoons made from reindeer-antler, and bone handles for the tanged points. One of these handles is decorated with a purely ornamental design, in strong contrast with the naturalistic tendencies of Magdalenian art.

The study of the reindeer skeletons found at Meiendorf proves that these animals were hunted with harpoons. Other

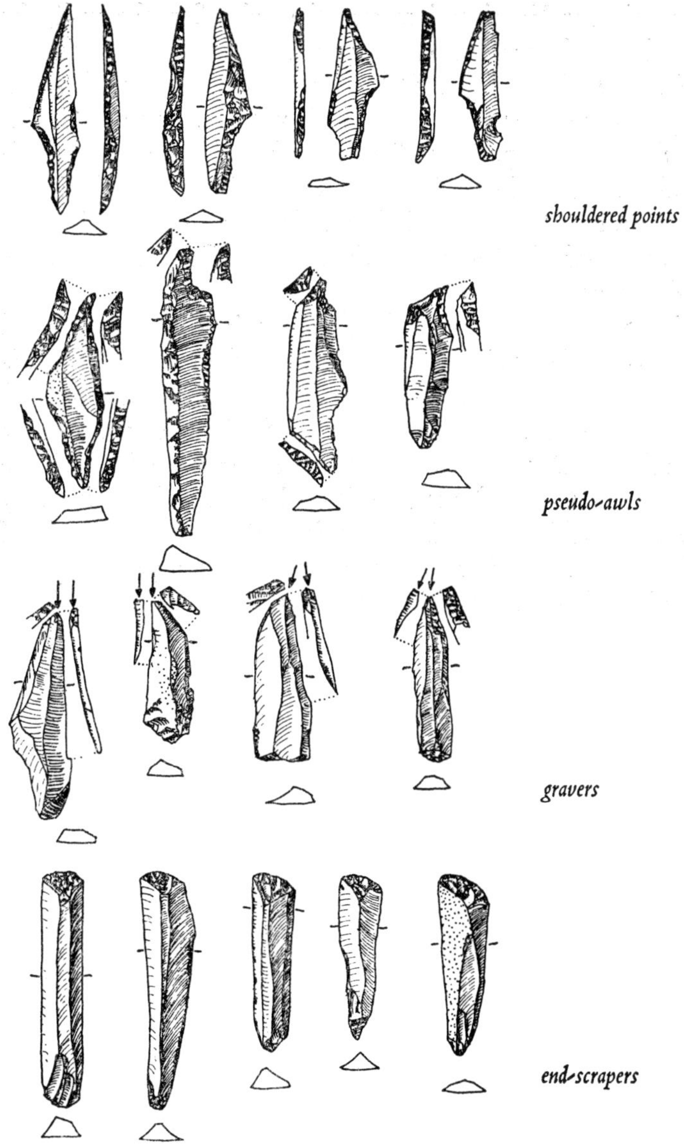

shouldered points

pseudo-awls

gravers

end-scrapers

Fig. 11. *Hamburgian implements from Ureterp (Frisia), 2:1*

game for the Hamburgians was the polar fox, the wolf, the wild horse, the wolverine, the swan and the white grouse.

In the Meiendorf and Stellmoor peat-bogs several skeletons of young reindeer were discovered, with heavy stones inside the thoracic cavity. These finds have been interpreted as sacrificial remains: at the beginning of the hunting season, the Hamburgians killed a young reindeer and threw the carcass into the pool near which they were living, as an offering to the spirits of the chase.

Up to now no trace of the Hamburgians had been found south of the large rivers passing through the Netherlands. It is not impossible, however, that certain contacts may have existed between the Hamburgian people and the Magdalenians living in Belgium. A recently discovered site near Mons (Bois-Saint-Macaire at Obourg) has revealed a late palaeolithic industry characterized by strong Hamburgian influences. The study of this deposit is still in its first stage, and it is too early to give a definite opinion about this particular site.

CHAPTER III

Mesolithic Food-gatherers

THE TRANSITION FROM the Upper Palaeolithic to the Mesolithic was a very gradual one. In fact, no fundamental difference exists between the mode of life of upper palaeolithic and mesolithic man: both live exclusively from hunting, fishing, the gathering of edible roots and the picking of wild fruit. Nevertheless, the climatic changes following the end of the glacial period strongly influenced the natural habitat of man living in our regions at that period; the evolution of fauna and flora was certainly most drastic. Man had to adapt himself to these different circumstances, as is apparent from the profound changes in his equipment. This progressive adaptation is reflected in the different mesolithic cultures which succeeded one another during the seven or eight millennia over which this period extended in the Low Countries. Before treating them separately, however, it is necessary to sketch briefly the evolution of the natural environment.

Six main climatic periods have been distinguished by geologists and palynologists between the end of the last glaciation and the present day. Only the first four interest us for the moment. The first, the Subarctic period, is not very different from the last glacial phase. The climate has not changed very much; the land is covered with a tundra vegetation, with here and there a few birches and pine trees; the fauna is still the same. This period, however, dating approximately between 13,000 and 8000 B.C., was interrupted by a warmer phase, the 'Allerød oscillation', which lasted for about one thousand years (tenth millennium B.C. (?)), characterized by the appearance of rather dense pine forests. This milder phase was followed by a return of cold and tundra, with pine and birch. The Subarctic can therefore be divided into three phases: the older Dryas, the Allerød oscillation and the younger Dryas. The older Dryas still belongs to the Palaeolithic: it is the period of the younger Magdalenian and Hamburgian. We will therefore consider the Allerød oscillation as the starting-point of the Mesolithic, though a conventional one, the transition between palaeolithic and mesolithic cultures having been very gradual.

The younger Dryas was succeeded by the Preboreal, lasting only for a short time: about one thousand years according to some geologists (8000–7000 B.C.), five hundred at the most, according to others. During this period, the temperature rose rapidly. It has been calculated that the average July temperature rose from 8° C. (46° F.) to 12° C. (53° F.). Pine forests and birch reappear, and towards the end of the period hazel is found. The frozen subsoil (*tjäle*) gradually thaws out, and peat-bogs develop in the low-lying regions or on top of the impenetrable subsoil (like the Fagnes). The whole region between England and the Low Countries becomes marshy. Evidence for the faunal changes come, for example, from the Remouchamps cave, dating from this period. One still finds steppe and tundra animals (reindeer, arctic hare, white grouse, arctic fox, wild horse), but also forest-dwellers (wild boar, aurochs, red deer).

During the Boreal—a dry period lasting from about 7000 to 5000 B.C.—the temperature still rose. The average July temperature, 12° C. (53° F.) to 14° C. (57° F.) at the beginning of the Boreal, rises to 16° C. (61° F.) at the end of this phase, a temperature almost corresponding to our present-day average. It was, however, a more continental climate than today. While on the low-lying land the formation of peat-bogs continues, the flora is characterized by pine forests with hazel scrub. Oak, lime, elm and alder appear. The fauna is characterized by animals living in the forests: elk, aurochs, red deer, roe-buck, wild boar, fox, beaver, otter, etc. The gradual melting of the ice-cap caused the sea-level to rise slowly, and about 5000 B.C.

the coastal strip of Belgium and the western part of the Netherlands as far as a line joining Bergen-op-Zoom to Groningen,
over Utrecht, Stavoren and Leeuwarden, are completely
covered by the sea. A large coastal lagoon is formed in these
submerged regions by deposition of sand and silt.

About 5000 B.C. begins the Atlantic period, lasting till
about 1500 B.C., and comprising both the end of the Mesolithic
and the whole of the Neolithic. The climate has become humid,
but the temperature is even higher than before and reaches an
optimal July average of about 18° C. (64° F.). The continuous
rise in the sea-level causes the rupture of the Pas-de-Calais—
definitely separating the British Isles from the Continent—and
the flooding of the low-lying country between North Sea and
Baltic. The coastal dunes along the Belgian and Dutch shores,
separating part of the lagoon from the sea, are formed by the
action of the North Sea tides provoked by all these phenomena.
This part of the coastal lagoon changes into a marshy region,
occasionally flooded by the sea where new peat deposits
are formed. The flora is characterized—mainly in the higher-
lying parts—by the mixed oak forest (oak, lime, elm, ash, with
hazel scrub locally), while in the plains alder predominates.
The fauna has changed little since the previous period, but
aurochs and elk have become very scarce.

Mesolithic man has had to adapt himself to this ecological
evolution. In the cultural development of this archaeological
period, three successive stages can be distinguished, the first
corresponding to the Allerød oscillation, the younger Dryas
and the Preboreal, the second to the Boreal, and the third to
the Atlantic. In each of these stages it will be necessary to distinguish between several civilizations, the differences resulting
at the same time from divergent ancestral traditions and from
the adaptation to a different natural habitat.

Some of the Mesolithic I cultures find their origin in the upper palaeolithic civilizations of our regions, the others being formed by the arrival of new elements in the population. We will make a distinction between the Epimagdalenian Tjonger group—originating in the English Creswellian, the Epimagdalenian group from south Belgium—which seems to be the continua′ tion of the Belgian Magdalenian, and the Ahrensburg civiliza′ tion, issuing from the Hamburgian. A few mixed sites will have to be considered separately, while lastly something will be said about the problem of the Prototardenoisian in the Low Countries.

The Hamburgian culture represented the first invasion into the regions of North′western Europe newly freed from ice; during the Allerød oscillation it was followed by a second in′ vasion, coming this time—it seems—from southern and central England, which at the time still were part of the Continent. We find the civilization of these new′comers in northern Bel′ gium and in the Netherlands, where it is known as the 'Tjonger group' (Tjonger being the name of a river in Frisia). The most important sites are situated in Frisia (Prandinge, Donkerbroek, Makkinga, Kjellingen, Appelsga, Houtige′ hage), Drenthe (Gees, Hullen), Guelders (Elspeet), Overijssel (the best excavated site: Usselo, near Enschede), northern Brabant (Drunen, Budel) and Belgian Limburg (Lommel, Zolder). Most of these sites are situated near a watercourse on sandy soil; it may be supposed that they represent camps of hunters or fishermen. The best known site, at Usselo, was situated on a promontory surrounded on three sides by a lake and marshes. In the habitation layer, a number of hearths and flint′chipping floors have been found, some of which were situated in shallow pits dug into the soil. The most typical of the flint implements are Gravette′points and Gravette′blades (most of all, small blades with blunted back, the so′called 'pen′knives'). These points and blades are rather different

from the upper palaeolithic Gravette types: they are more irregular and less finely made, the back being rounded or carinated.
Several upper palaeolithic types of burins are found, round

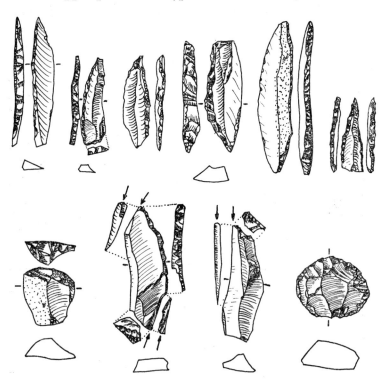

*Fig. 12. Implements of the Tjonger group, from Usselo near Enschede
(prov. Overijssel), 2:3.*

scrapers and scrapers on blades—simple or double—often
short and heavy, already announcing the mesolithic scrapers.
Shoulder points do not occur. The industry therefore is quite
different from the Hamburgian or its mesolithic derivative, the
Ahrensburgian (cf. *infra*). It must be noted, however, that at
Usselo one shouldered point and two pseudo-awls were found,

Fig 1.

indicating contacts between the Hamburgian and the Tjonger people. Since both groups lived in the same region, this is not surprising. The Tjonger group is clearly related—apart from some differences—to the Epimagdalenian cultures of north-western Germany: the 'Rissen group' and the 'Wehlen group'.[1] The problem of the origin of this culture is a complicated one. Geological and palynological studies, made in Belgium, the Netherlands and Germany, give a date in the Allerød oscillation and the beginning of the younger Dryas; therefore it cannot belong to the Aurignacian, as has been said by several typologically-minded archaeologists. In the Aurignacian, the combination of round-backed Gravette-points with short and heavy scrapers does not exist. No genetic relationship with the Hamburgian can be found, while the classic French Magdalenian is also excluded. Other Magdalenian groups, however, had kept the Gravette-points and blades, notably the English Creswellian, in which strong Aurignacian influences can be found, notwithstanding its final Magdalenian date. It is therefore very probable that the origin of the Tjonger group must be sought in the Creswellian, while in the Rissen and Wehlen groups influences from the Creswellian and the late Magdalenian from Rhineland-Westphalia and from south-eastern Germany are combined. The Tjonger group seems to be contemporaneous with the later phases of the Hamburgian (Usselo), but it is older than the Ahrensburgian which is palynologically dated as belonging to the younger Dryas. At Rissen, near Hamburg, the Ahrensburgian was found above the Epimagdalenian level.

Special mention must be made of a third Belgian site: Zonhoven. Two stratigraphically defined mesolithic levels were discovered on top of each other. The upper layer represents a late Tardenoisian dating from the Atlantic period; the lower level has for a long time been considered as a Prototardenoisian, characterized by very simple microliths: obliquely blunted

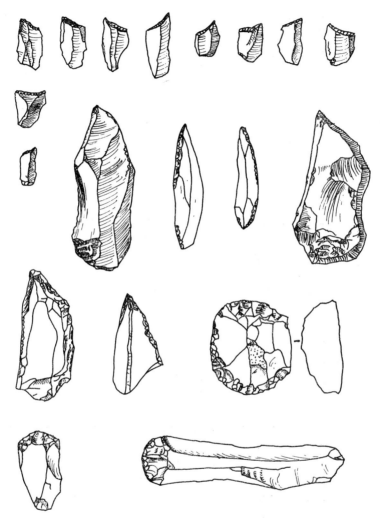

Fig. 13. Mesolithic implements from the lower level at Zonhoven (Belgian Limburg), 2:3.

points—the so-called 'Zonhoven-points'—points blunted down the whole of one edge, and triangles. Some of the Zonhoven points have been trimmed at the base. More recent excavations have given a more complete picture of this industry. Together with these microliths, a certain number of Gravette-points have been found, with burins, round scrapers and scrapers on blades, some short and massive, without lateral retouching. The Zonhoven site combines the characteristics of the Tjonger group with a microlithic industry.

Fig. 13

During the younger Dryas, the Hamburgian traditions were continued in the Ahrensburg culture, known mainly from north-west German sites, for instance the higher levels at Stell-moor. From the Netherlands three sites have been reported: at Vessem and Geldrop in North Brabant, and at Montfort in Limburg. Only a lithic industry has been discovered there, but the German peat-bogs have yielded a much more complete picture of this culture. The lithic industry is characterized by tanged points, smaller and more delicately finished than the final Hamburgian ones, but without a doubt deriving from these. They were used as arrow-heads: at Stellmoor one has been found, still attached to its wooden shaft. A few obliquely blunted points of Zonhoven type (*supra*) were also discovered. Lastly may be noted the abundance of simple and double scrapers, often short and massive, the numerous crudely re-touched large blades, and the complete absence of pseudo-awls. Numerous traces of worked reindeer-antler were found at Stell-moor, the most characteristic pieces being the 'Lyngby axes', the oldest axes now known, and proving the necessity for man to adapt his equipment to an environment in which the forest occupies an ever-increasing area. Retouching implements, scrapers made from reindeer collar-bone, piercers, harpoons and arrow-heads are found. Like their Hamburgian ancestors, the Ahrensburg people made reindeer sacrifices and certain facts seem to indicate that reindeer-skulls were fixed on poles stuck into the earth. The Ahrensburg culture derives indubitably from the Hamburgian, but certain influences from the Swiderian from Eastern Europe and from microlithic industries—of

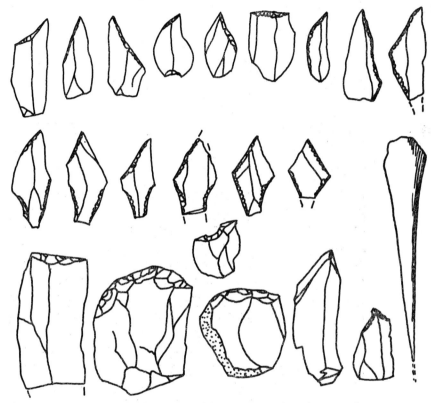

Fig. 14. Stone and bone industry from the Remouchamps cave, actual size (prov. Liège).

which more later—are apparent. The Ahrensburgian dates from the younger Dryas, following the Allerød oscillation.

The industry discovered in the Remouchamps cave (prov. Liège, Belgium) is closely related to the Ahrensburgian, but the microlithic element is more pronounced. Two hearths were found in the cave, in a level containing implements and

Plate 6

Fig. 14

remains of meals; inside a crevice in the wall, part of a dis-turbed burial was discovered: a few finger-bones and human teeth, together with a necklace made of about forty perforated shells. The lithic industry is a flake industry, with a large proportion of microliths: Zonhoven points, tanged points and irregular triangles are numerous. A few transverse arrow-heads and points blunted down the whole of one edge have been found, together with one burin and some discoid scrapers. Micro-burins do not exist. The bone industry consists of three piercers and one piece of polished bone, decorated by clusters of five shallow pits. The fauna, the composition of which has been given earlier, shows that the Remouchamps site is approxi-mately of the same age as the Ahrensburg civilization. In front of the cave was found an open-air station, the 'station Leduc', yielding a similar series of artefacts; at a depth of 2 ft. 7 in. under the actual surface, i.e. 7 ft. 10 in. above the level of the Amblève, nine hearths were found of about 4 ft. 11 in. diameter and lying on top of circular pebble platforms. The Remouchamps in-dustry represents a combination of the Ahrensburgian, of which it has the typical tanged points, with a microlithic element strongly reminiscent of the Zonhoven site. It may be noted that the decoration of the bone reminds one of certain motifs found in the Maglemosean (Mesolithic II). The presence of numerous perforated fossil mollusc-shells of the Paris region (*natica parisiensis* and *melania lactea*), however, makes one think of similar finds in Belgian Magdalenian sites (cf. *supra*).

A third Mesolithic I industry is found in southern Belgium, in a series of caves and open-air deposits, mainly in the pro-vinces of Namur, Hainaut, Luxembourg, Liège and Brabant. The stone industry is of Magdalenian tradition, but with numerous microliths. Implements made from reindeer-antler have to some extent taken the place of the reindeer-antler arte-facts. Unfortunately, these sites have not been studied very carefully, and it is quite possible that at least some of them—

like the caves at Châleux and Montaigle (prov. Namur) and at La Préalle near Heyd (prov. Luxembourg)—may be related to the Remouchamps site. The Azilian, which in France has its origin in the Magdalenian, has not yet been found in the Low Countries.

A last problem to be mentioned is the origin of the micro-liths, found in all the already mentioned industries. Although microliths do exist in very small numbers as early as the Aurig-nacian, it seems that their presence in the Mesolithic I indus-tries must be explained by the influence of immigrants. The same types of microliths are found in such different industries as the Tjonger group (Zonhoven), the Ahrensburgian (Re-mouchamps), and the Epimagdalenian of southern Belgium: Zonhoven points, points blunted down the whole of one edge and triangles. Can they be Prototardenoisian? As long as no typical Prototardenoisian site has been dug in the Low Coun-tries it will be difficult to give an opinion on this subject.

It appears that the Mesolithic I cultures present rather ill-defined and very variable characteristics; they show the efforts of man to adapt himself gradually to his changing environ-ment. In the Boreal phase, this adaptation is completed, and two important Mesolithic II cultures emerge in the Low Countries: the Maglemosean and the Tardenoisian, each of which represents the equipment of people living in entirely different surroundings. Indeed, the Maglemosean sites are situated in regions which, in Boreal times, were covered with forests, and near lakes, marshes and rivers. The Tardenoisian people, on the contrary, have clearly avoided the forest; traces of their culture are found on dry soils, covered only with scrub vegetation.

The Maglemosean culture covers a very large area, comprising almost the whole of the North European plain, from England

D

(the land-bridge with the Continent still existing) in the West, to Poland in the East; from southern Norway and southern Sweden in the North to Flanders and northern France (Artois and Picardy) in the South. It seems even to be related, at least as far as concerns the bone and antler industry, to the Kunda-culture of Esthonia. Apart from certain local aspects, it shows a remarkable cultural unity in this vast territory. The centre of expansion of this civilization must be sought in Denmark (Sjaelland) and in southern Sweden (Skåne and Blekinge), where most of the sites are concentrated. The majority of the excavated stations are situated near lakes, marshes or rivers; they were summer camps, generally flooded during the winter. The traces of the Maglemosean culture have been admirably preserved by the conditions of humidity in the marshy soil. The localization of the settlements near the water, the remains of the meals and the equipment itself prove that the Magle-moseans lived in small groups, subject to seasonal migrations, and lived mainly from fishing, hunting—waterfowl and forest game—and wild fruit. In the remains of their meals one finds fishbones and the bones of wild duck, goose, swan, aurochs, elk, wild boar, red deer and roe-buck. For the first time in history man had found a new companion, the dog, the first animal to be domesticated, and a valuable aid in tracking down game in forested areas. In the lithic industry, apart from a few artefacts derived from types already known in upper palaeolithic times (burins, scrapers, piercers), two typical elements can be distinguished: first of all, a series of microliths borrowed by Magle-mosean man from the Tardenoisian civilization of this period (points blunted down the whole of one edge; Zonhoven points, isosceles and scalene triangles, a few micro-burins), and used partly as arrow-heads, partly as elements of composite imple-ments (e.g. barbs inserted into wooden or bone shafts); secondly, a series of heavy woodworking implements, indica-ting an adaptation of Maglemosean man to a forest habitat (axes, adzes, chisels, picks of core-type and the so-called flake-axes (*grand tranchet*)). Arrows and handles for implements were made of wood; a dug-out canoe and a few paddles are known. The marshy soil has even preserved fragments of fishing nets, made of plaited bark-fibres of certain plants; to these nets were attached pine-bark floaters and sinkers made of perforated stones. Axes and adzes made of red deer antler and bone have been found, together with implement handles in antler, and bone daggers, piercers, needles and barbless fishhooks. Lastly —the most important Maglemosean fossil—numerous bone and antler points of various types (notched points, single-barbed points, points with one or two series of barbs, points with inserted flint barbs, etc.), of which some may have been used as harpoons, but of which the majority were used as fish-prongs or bird-arrows.

This very complete picture of the life and equipment of the small Maglemosean groups has been made possible by the systematic excavation of Scandinavian and English sites, but the unity of the Maglemosean civilization may perhaps allow us to extend this picture to our own regions, though no Magle-mosean settlement has yet been dug in Belgium or in the Nether-lands, and only stray finds—and rather poor ones at that—prove the existence of this culture in the Low Countries. No flint implements have been recognized, very probably because the isolated microliths have been attributed to the Tardenoisian, and the heavier equipment (axes, etc.) have up to now not been found to belong to the Maglemosean. In the Netherlands, only one harpoon with a single series of barbs made from red deer antler has been discovered near Emmen in Drenthe; a series of fossil Boreal skulls, some of which were found together with worked red deer antler (Hengelo, Koerhuisbeek, Zandweert, Deventer) have been attributed to the Maglemosean. In Bel-gium, the finds, more numerous and more typical, are concen-trated in the region of the River Scheldt and some of its tributaries (Rupel, Dyle, Dender, Haine). About twenty bone or red deer antler points are known, mostly with one series of barbs—the Kunda type (Schoonaarde, Willebroek, Malines, Appels, Hamme, Zele, Heusden, Melle, Ninove, Pom-meroeuil, Maisières, Obourg, etc.). It is possible that certain other finds from these same regions, e.g. a few bone daggers, red deer antler picks, bone piercers and hooks, may belong to the Maglemosean, but this is much less certain. The marshy Scheldt valley seems to have suited Maglemosean man very well indeed. In the other parts of Belgium, no trace of this civilization has been discovered. On the other hand, the Tardenoisian sites are very numerous.

The problem of the origin of the Tardenoisian culture, which, during the Boreal and part of the Atlantic period, covered most of Western and Central Europe, is too complex to be discussed here. Was it imported by North African and Syrian immigrants, whom we have called the 'Prototarde-noisians'? Was it a simple evolution of upper palaeolithic and epipalaeolithic civilizations? Or must a combination of both possibilities be considered? Personally we are rather in favour of this last hypothesis. Be that as it may, the Tardenoisian sites are abundant, both in the Netherlands and in Belgium, and it would be too much to name them all. They are found mostly outside the forested areas. In highland Belgium they are nearly always situated on the exposed plateaux, next to the valleys of the Meuse tributaries (mainly the Amblève, Ourthe and Vesdre), generally near a spring. In central and lowland Belgium and in the Netherlands, the Tardenoisian sites are found in the sandy regions, near a small watercourse or a lake; the stations are very numerous in Campine and in northern Brabant, in Twenthe, in Drenthe and in the Veluwe, but also in several other places. The main food supply seems to have come from fishing and small-game hunting. In highland Bel-gium a few settlements are known from caves and rock-shelters,

Plate 8

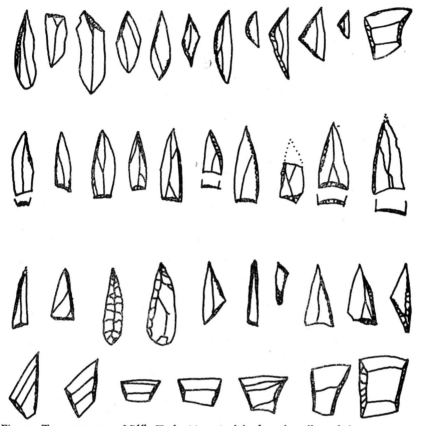

Fig. 15. Two upper rows: Middle Tardenoisian microliths from the valleys of the Amblève, the Ourthe and the Vesdre.
Two lower rows: Upper Tardenoisian microliths from Zonhoven (Belgian Limburg).
Actual size.

but most of the sites are open-air stations. Traces of huts have been discovered at Sougné (near the River Amblève), at Wegnez (near the River Vesdre) and at La Roche aux Faucons (near the River Ourthe): shallow circular or oval pits, about 16 to 27 in. deep, with a diameter of 6½ to 9¾ ft., and with fragments of the wattle and daub walls. Traces of hearths, remains of meals and numerous flint chippings were found. Similar habitations have been excavated at Haule (Frisia). The sandy and acid soil has preserved only the stone industry, while bone, wood and antler material has perished. This stone industry is almost exclusively microlithic. Typologically—and, in one case, at Zonhoven, stratigraphically—two stages in the development of the Tardenoisian have been distinguished: the Middle Tardenoisian, dating from the Boreal, and the Upper Tardenoisian, dating from the Atlantic. Apart from the simple microliths already found in the Mesolithic I cultures (Zonhoven points, points blunted down the whole of one edge), the Middle Tardenoisian is characterized by smaller and more regular triangles than those of the preceding period, crescents, lozenges, points with concave base and already a few trapezes. Flint-working 'débris' also occurs: thin flakes, nuclei and micro-burins. A few bigger implements are found: burins, convex scrapers, hammer-stones and anvils. The typical Maglemosean heavy woodworking equipment is absent. The Upper Tardenoisian has the same artefacts, but the trapezes become the most important type, while lanceate points also occur. These microliths formed part of composite implements, and were used, for instance, as barbs. The trapezes (*petits tranchets*) seem to have been used mainly as transverse arrow-heads. The Belgian Tardenoisian does perhaps reveal the modest beginnings of trade relations: indeed, on numerous sites in Belgium and the southern part of the Netherlands, many microliths in Wommersom quartzite have been found, and only one outcrop of this stone is known in the Low Countries: at Wommersom, near Tirlemont.[2]

Fig. 15

The Upper Tardenoisian has brought us to the Mesolithic III. This culture lasted for many centuries, probably even during the whole of the Neolithic: while the first farmers—to be discussed later—were already firmly established on the lands suitable for their primitive form of agriculture, the Tardenoisian people continued to live in the sandy regions, following their ancestral traditions and undergoing no influence, or very little, from the first neolithic civilizations. Proof of this is given by the upper level at Zonhoven, where trapezes have been found, made from fragments of neolithic polished axes.

Mention must be made here of the most spectacular meso-lithic discovery of recent years: near Pesse (Drenthe), an almost three-metre-long fire-hollowed canoe, made of a pine-trunk, was found. Radiocarbon readings indicate an age of almost 8000 years (i.e. 6000 B.C.); this allows us to place this boat in the Mesolithic II period.

Plate 7

If the Mesolithic III is characterized in many regions by the Upper Tardenoisian, traces of other cultures belonging to the same period have been found in other places.

In Northern Europe, the Maglemosean gradually gives way to the Ertebølle culture. The transitional stage, the so-called Oldesloe culture, found mainly in Schleswig-Holstein, is known in the Netherlands from the site of Zwartveen (Smal-lingerland, Frisia) where a heavy stone industry, adapted for woodwork, has been discovered: roughly-made axes, *tranchets*, together with discoid scrapers and microliths, amongst these many trapezes. The excavation has yielded traces of two huts, about $6\frac{1}{2}$ ft. in diameter. Pollen analysis has placed this site in the early Atlantic.

The Scandinavian Ertebølle culture and the Lower Halstow culture of south-eastern England, related to the first, and also derived from the Maglemosean, are not represented in the Low Countries. However, near the Dutch frontier, in the north of the province of Liège, at Aubel, Fouron-Saint-Martin, Fouron-Saint-Pierre and Remersdaal, a series of sites has been dis-covered, the lithic industry of which is certainly related to the two civilizations mentioned above, and very probably deriving from these. This culture has been given the name of Campignian, but its characteristics are more archaic than those of the classic French Campignian. For this reason, together with several other archaeologists, we prefer the name of 'Precampignian'. The French sites which most resemble the Belgian ones, are those of the Forest of Fontainebleau and Montmorency; the artefacts there were made of sandstone, whereas those from Belgium are made of flint. All the Belgian sites show the same characteristics: one finds funnel-shaped pits, 6 to 10 ft. deep, for the extraction of flint. The artefacts were made on the spot and the pits gradually filled in with the chippings. All these implements are heavy, massive and roughly flaked. The two most typical are the *grand tranchet*, generally triangular in shape and of which the cutting edge is formed by the oblique intersection of two flake scars; and the long pick, with subtriangular section. One also finds spherical and pyramidal throwing stones, scrapers, piercers, hammer-stones, and strange heavy implements with a flat base, the so-called 'flat-irons',

Fig. 16

which may have been used for removing the flesh from hides. All these implements are crudely flaked and have a very unfinished aspect. It will be noted that axes do not occur. A few sherds of very coarse pottery have been found on these sites, but it is thought that they are later in date and cannot therefore be attributed to the Campignian.

Some archaeologists have tried to place the Belgian Campignian in the Neolithic, but nothing indicates that this view is correct. There is no proof that these people were farmers or bred cattle, nor that they were in any way acquainted with other neolithic inventions, like making pottery or polishing flint. On the contrary, everything seems to indicate that they lived from fishing, hunting, and food gathering, like their cousins the Ertebølle people or the people from the Lower Halstow culture. The chronological position of the Belgian Precampignian,

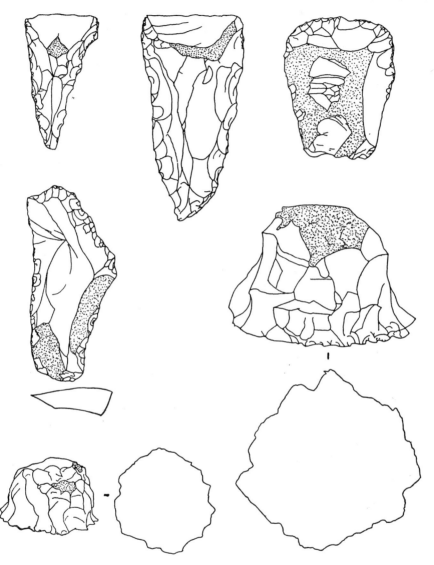

Fig. 16. Precampignian implements from Aubel (prov. Liège), 1:2.

however, poses certain problems. Like the Ertebølle, it dates from the Atlantic period, and is—in Belgium—certainly older than the Michelsberg civilization, where one finds definite Campignian influences in the stone industry. On the other hand, no analogies can be found with the Danubian Neolithic, which in our regions occupies the same area as the Campignian. The following chapter will show that the first neolithic invasion in the Low Countries was only an interlude touching a small area of the country, while everywhere else the mesolithic mode of life continued. These first agriculturists only stayed here for a relatively short time, and after their departure a long and purely mesolithic period continued. It is not impossible that the Campignian, although a mesolithic culture, is chronologically later than this first neolithic invasion.

The Campignian people almost industrialized flint extraction. It will be shown later that at Spiennes the Michelsberg people also specialized in the working of the flint-mines; their equipment is very similar to that of the Campignians. Apart from the Spiennes mines, other sites for the extraction of flint are known, some of which seem to be more archaic than Spiennes (e.g. Obourg). It remains to be seen whether the earliest efforts in flint exploitation in the Mons region and in Dutch Limburg (Rijckholt-Sint-Geertruid), must not be attributed to the Campignian people. Not enough is known yet about these sites to give a definite opinion on the subject. The flint-mines will be discussed in more detail in a later chapter.

CHAPTER IV

The First Agricultural Communities

URING THE TIME when in Europe the second Mesolithic Period flourished, a new stage in the evolution of
mankind started in the Near East: slowly man began to under-
stand the first principles of agriculture and succeeded in taming
some species of animal which provided him with milk, meat,
wool and hides. By producing a certain part of his food by his
own labour, he, for the first time in history, became less
dependent upon the nature of his immediate surroundings. The
first signs of this cultural revolution, with its incalculable
consequences, go back at least to the seventh millennium B.C.[1]
Instead of having to be satisfied with what he could get and to
adapt himself in order to survive, as heretofore, man gradually
began to control and to transform Nature according to his own
needs. He now lived an almost sedentary life near his fields, in
villages where social life and the laws which regulated it
gradually took shape. Because of this, he made rapid progress
in many technical domains: weaving linen and wool became
known, pottery-making was invented, and the use of the wheel
made transport much more rapid and easy. These first agricultural communities, where social and craft specializations
rapidly came into being, form the basis of true civilization
which from this moment onwards progressed with ever-
increasing speed.

However, it will be centuries and even millennia before the
first indications of this 'neolithic revolution' become visible in
Western Europe, and even then in a very attenuated form.

It was near the end of the fifth millennium that the first
mixed farming communities, coming from the East, settled in
the Netherlands, and a little later in Belgium.[2] This civilization
had already been recognized in Belgium in 1888 and was

called the 'Omalian' (from the village of Omal, near Liège). This name is still frequently used, even though it has been known for a long time that the Omalian is part of the so-called 'Danubian' complex. The centre of this culture is situated in Moravia, Bohemia and the adjacent region of central Germany, but its dispersion area covers practically the whole of Central Europe. However, since the Dutch-Belgian group presents certain distinctive characteristics—although closely related to the Rhenish group of Plaidt-Cologne—the use of the name 'Omalian' is still justified.

Only the most primitive forms of cultivation were known to the Danubian farmers. They used hoes to work the soil, but were still ignorant of plough or fertilizer. For these reasons they had to keep to a certain type of soil. Sandy soils were too infertile, and clay too heavy to be worked with their primitive implements. The distribution map of the Danubian settlements in Central Europe therefore corresponds very closely with the loess areas. This explains why in the Low Countries traces of this civilization are to be found only in Dutch Limburg and in Belgian Hesbaye. During the Atlantic period, these loess areas were covered with mixed oak forest, which was cleared by the slash and burn method wherever the Danubian farmers wanted to start cultivating new fields. These fields were exhausted after a rather short time, because of the lack of manure and the shallow surface digging. The land was then left fallow and the people started afresh elsewhere, sometimes, after a number of years, returning to their first plot, which, by a process of natural rejuvenation, had become fertile again. This very slow semi-nomadism explains at the same time the extensive distribution area of the Danubian culture, and its considerable uniformity throughout the loess lands.

Coming from the region of Cologne, groups of Danubian farmers arrived in the Meuse valley in Dutch Limburg and settled there. About ten villages have up to now been discovered, of which a few are certainly older than the Omalian settlements in Belgian Hesbaye. Most of these Dutch villages are situated on the right bank of the River Meuse (only Caberg is on the left bank). After staying in Dutch Limburg for some time, a number of these newcomers crossed the River Meuse and moved further to the south. Following the Jeker valley, they colonized part of Hesbaye, between the River Jeker to the north, the River Méhaigne to the south and the River Meuse to the east. Although it did not last for a very long time (cf. *infra*), this Omalian incursion supported a rather important number of people. Indeed, more than twenty villages are known from Hesbaye, some of which were certainly bigger than Köln-Lindenthal, made famous by the excavations of W. Buttler and W. Haberey.

Until very recently, most of these Omalian sites in Belgium had been dug in a rather haphazard way, the excavators being satisfied with collecting the lithic material and the pottery found in the rubbish pits, which were interpreted as '*fonds de cabanes*' (pit dwellings). On the other hand, excavations in the Netherlands, namely at Caberg, Stein, and more recently at Elslo, Sittard and Geleen, together with the systematic and very recent work done at the Belgian site of Rosmeer, are more satisfactory and have shown that the Danubian villages of our regions are very similar to the type-site at Köln-Lindenthal. However, since none of these villages have been wholly exca-vated, the picture they present must be completed with what is known from the Rhenish sites.

Some villages, like the earliest settlement at Köln-Lindenthal, had not been fortified; others, like the earliest village of Sittard, were at least partly surrounded with a palisade, while the second occupation period of this site shows no trace of fortifications (it remains to be seen whether the palisade was used as a forti-fication, or must be interpreted as a cattle enclosure). At Stein, where two villages, belonging to different periods, were discovered close together, the older one was not fortified, while the more recent settlement was perhaps surrounded with a rampart.

In all these villages, the houses do not seem to be placed according to a fixed plan, although generally they face the same direction. They are rectangular, 16 to 23 ft. wide and with a length varying between 26 and 115 ft. Plan and method of construction are variable. In the interior, one finds generally traces of three parallel rows of posts supporting a saddle-roof. In some cases the exterior walls were made by uprights placed at regular distances, the intervals being filled with wattle and daub. Mostly, however, one of the short sides and the bigger half of the long sides were made with squared tree-trunks placed in a narrow foundation trench. This is mostly the case for the north-easterly part of the house, which is most exposed to the cold. In some exceptional cases, all four walls are made entirely with wooden uprights placed side by side. Lastly, certain smaller buildings (about 16 × 26 ft.) show traces of numerous posts placed very close together, so that almost no room exists between them big enough to live in: they probably are small barns built on piles to prevent moisture and rodents from damaging the harvest. Here and there between the houses one finds shallow or deeper pits, irregular in shape, where the inhabitants of the village dug the clay used for plastering the walls of their habitations. These pits, which formerly were erroneously interpreted as dwelling-pits, were used as rubbish dumps, and large quantities of stone implements and pottery sherds are found in them. Some of them the Omalian people used as open-air flint-working sites, while others probably were pigsties.

Three cereals were cultivated: *triticum monococcum, triticum dicoccum* and wheat, grains of which have been found in rubbish pits at Jeneffe and Oudoumont, and the imprints of which can be seen on some pottery sherds. In all Omalian villages, quite

Fig. 17

Fig. 18

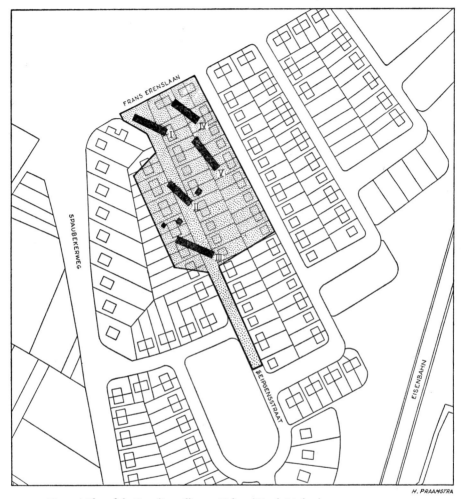

Fig. 17. Plan of the Danubian village at Geleen (Dutch Limburg).

a large number of sandstone querns have been discovered. Proof of the existence of the weaving technique is given by sherds from Jeneffe, where the ornamentation consists of textile impressions.

We know much less about domesticated animals, because loess conditions are not favourable for the preservation of bones. In a few Omalian sites, however, bones and teeth from ox, sheep, goat and pig have been found. Apart from cattle-breeding and agriculture, hunting continued to play its part in the alimentation of Omalian man, and the site at Liège has yielded bones of red deer, wild boar, birds and fishes.

One of the most characteristic fossils of the Danubian civilization is its pottery. First of all one finds coarse and plain vessels: hemispherical bowls and large provision jars with rounded base, with or without neck and with massive prehension knobs, some horizontally, others vertically perforated. More typical is the finer and carefully smoothed ware, decorated with incisions cut into the unbaked clay. These small pots—at the most 4–6 in. high—are mostly spherical in form. The wavy or angular incised lines are very often parallel (this is the origin of the name 'Bandkeramik'), and had originally a filling of white or red colouring matter, of which traces can sometimes be seen. The stratigraphy of Köln-Lindenthal has enabled W. Buttler to study the typological evolution of this pottery. A few villages from Dutch Limburg (e.g. the first periods of Stein and Sittard and the villages of Geleen and Caberg) are characterized by the older type pottery (stages I and II of Köln-Lindenthal: *ältere Linearbandkeramik* and *jüngere Linearbandkeramik*), with rather simple decorations consisting of curved or angular parallel lines, sometimes forming meanders and spirals. Only a few points have sometimes been placed between two series of parallel lines. On the other hand, the pottery from the Belgian Hesbaye sites and from the younger sites from Dutch Limburg corresponds with stages III–IV of Köln-Lindenthal (*jüngste Linearbandkeramik*). The decoration is very rich and varied. Meanders, curves, spirals and lozenges are completely filled with dots, squares, or a network of parallel or transverse lines. A few pieces are of special

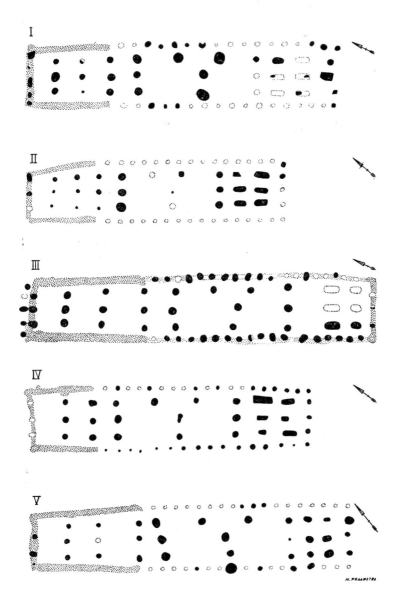

*Fig. 18. Plan of five habitations from the Danubian village at Geleen (Dutch Limburg).
I 105 ft. long, others to scale.*

Plates 9–12

interest, for instance the handle from Sittard shaped like a bovine head and which may be compared with a Moravian vase from the Brno Museum, and a few sherds from Jeneffe where the decoration is formed by the impression of a piece of woven cloth or very fine basketry work. A relief decoration made by fingertip impressions is found on certain sherds from Boirs and Wonck, and seems to be typical of the Belgian Omalian.

It is remarkable that the Danubian farmers from the Low Countries were still in contact with the groups from the Rhineland, as is proved by volcanic rock having been imported for the manufacture of certain implements, and by a degree of trade in pottery. Sherds decorated with fingertip impressions and coming from Hesbaye have been found in Köln-Lindenthal, while the site at Jeneffe has yielded pottery typical for the Plaidt region (Neuwied). Lastly, Hinkelstein ware (Worms region) has been discovered at Stein and Sittard. A Rössen pot was found at Stein, and at Sittard a fragment of a foot-bowl has come to light, similar to the type found at Jordansmühl. These last finds are very important for the relative chronology of the more recent phases of the Danubian in Dutch Limburg.

As regards the stone industry, the large quantities of flint implements on the Dutch and Belgian sites must be noted, which is in marked contrast with the scarcity of this material in the Rhineland. It has already been said that the flint was worked in the open-air stations established in the clay pits. Certain facts noted at Sittard and elsewhere seem to indicate that each village may have had its own specialist for the working of flint, who provided for the needs of the whole community. Apart from numerous nuclei and hammer-stones, this flint industry contains blades used for cutting and sawing, sickle blades fixed in wooden or bone handles and having a more or less denticulated edge with a very shiny area, due to the friction of the flint on

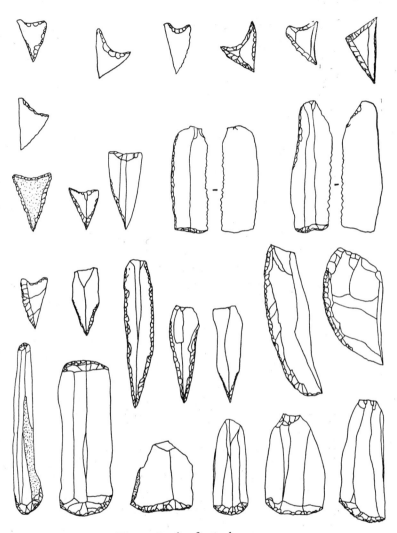

Fig. 19. Omalian flint implements, 1:2.

the stalks of the cereals. Endscrapers, piercers, triangular arrow/
heads with flat or concave base, and harpoon/barbs are found.
Fig. 19 These flint implements are never polished. We have already
mentioned the numerous sandstone querns. Very typical of the
Omalian are the implements made of hard or volcanic rock
(phtanite, tephrite, trachyte, basalt, etc.) which are polished,
Fig. 20 in contrast to the flint artefacts. Most typical of all are the shoe/
last celts with assymetrical profile which have often been inter/
preted as hoes. It is possible that some may indeed have served
this purpose, but it seems that Omalian man used mainly
wooden or antler hoes. The majority of these shoe/last celts
were chisels or adzes used in connection with woodwork. The
construction of wooden houses could explain the abundance of
these implements. There were, furthermore, perforated sand/
stone discs which may have been used as bolas, and heavy
hammers which probably served to smash the lumps of earth
after the soil had been turned over by the hoe. At least 85% of
the polished stone implements from the Belgian sites are made
of rocks which are not found in Belgium; the other 15% are
made from rocks existing in this country, but they could just
as well be imported. Only specimens made from phtanite are
almost certainly made from indigenous rock. The stones used
seem to come from the Eifel region, which is one more indica/
tion of the rather active trade relations existing between the
Danubians of the Low Countries and their Rhenish cousins.
These stones may have been imported as finished products, but
it is equally possible that the Omalian people themselves
polished them. A series of unfinished adzes and the discovery
of a few sandstone polishing stones show that at least some of
these implements were made in our own regions.

We know almost nothing of the bone and antler industries,
the loess being very unsuitable for the preservation of organic
material. However, the excavations under the Place Saint/
Lambert at Liège have yielded a small four/toothed bone comb,

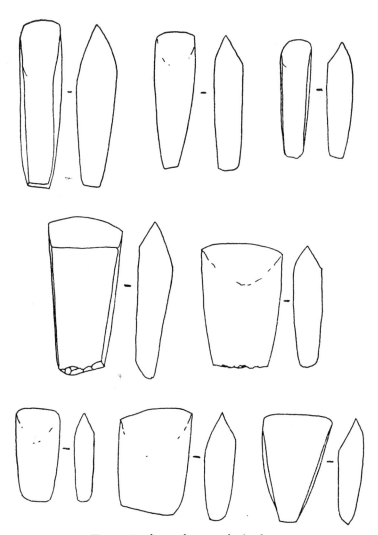

Fig. 20. Omalian implements in hard rock, 2:3.

used for tracing lines in pottery. The opposite end could have been used as an *ébauchoir* for shaping the pots. On the same site an object in antler has been found with one end perforated, the other sharpened and polished. It is probably a hoe. Very little is known also about the personal ornaments of the Omalian people. It may be noted, however, that quite a large number of sites have yielded haematite (oligiste) and other colouring matter in the form of small cakes or little sticks, or as powder. These pigments were probably used for painting the body and in connection with funeral rites.

A few words must be said about these funeral rites. In Central Europe, the Danubians buried their dead, mostly in individual tombs. Exceptional cases of cremation are known. It seems that the Omalian people practised this last ritual. Due to the bad preservation of bone in loess soil, only one cemetery has up to now been found, namely at Hollogne-aux-Pierres. The cremated bones, after having been sprinkled with haematite powder, were deposited in an oval grave. The grave-goods consisted of a few flint blades, an adze and a fragment of marcasite. Certain traces seem to indicate that the cremated bones were originally put into a wicker-work basket.

As has been shown earlier, the Danubian colonization of Dutch Limburg started a little before 4000 B.C. The colonization of Hesbaye was somewhat later and must be placed approximately at the beginning of the fourth millennium. The uniform character of the Omalian culture in Belgium in which no evolution can be distinguished, the abundance of implements made from foreign rock, the limitation of the colonized region to the eastern part of Hesbaye, while other loess areas were to be found more to the south-east—all this seems to indicate that the Danubian occupation of Belgium cannot have lasted very long, probably not exceeding two or three centuries. Perhaps the occupation of Dutch Limburg lasted a little longer, as the importation of pottery from the Hinkelstein,

Rössen and Jordansmühl cultures suggests. In the absence of radiocarbon readings from these last cultures, we will not risk an absolute date, particularly since other such readings have completely changed the chronology of the Danubian civiliza⁄ tions. The most we can say is that this occupation did not last later than the end of the fourth millennium. We know nothing about the reasons why the Danubians left the Low Countries.

This first neolithic incursion touched only a very limited area of Belgium and the Netherlands. It practically did not influence the mode of life of the inhabitants of the other regions of the Low Countries, and the mesolithic way of life persisted for a long time after the departure of these first farming communi⁄ ties. The area where the Danubians had been established was, after their departure, perhaps occupied by the Precampignian people, of whom we have already talked in the preceding chapter. Indeed, the Omalian civilization shows no traces at all of Precampignian influences, while these are very strong in the artefacts of the neolithic civilizations of the third mil⁄ lennium.

CHAPTER V

The Diffusion of the Neolithic Way of Life

URING ITS WESTWARD expansion, the Danubian civilization had reached and colonized only a relatively small area of the Low Countries, and had disappeared rather quickly without leaving very definite traces. It scarcely influenced the way of life of the inhabitants of the other parts of Belgium and the Netherlands who followed their mesolithic traditions during the whole of the Danubian phase, and even continued to do so for quite a few centuries after the departure of the first agriculturalists.

The real diffusion of the Neolithic in our regions, with its profound inherent economic and social changes, was due to a second invasion of neolithic immigrants which reached the Low Countries several centuries after the disappearance of the Omalian culture. These newcomers colonized the greater part of North-western Europe, having started from eastern Central Europe or even from European Russia, where their culture originated in a fusion of an autochthonous mesolithic substratum with Danubian elements coming from the South. Recent radiocarbon readings place their arrival at about 2800–2700 B.C. Two originally closely related, but afterwards clearly distinct civilizations find their origin in this migration: the Funnel-beaker culture and the Michelsberg culture. Both are represented in the Low Countries, the first one in the Netherlands, while the second one is found only in Belgium. Under the influence of these immigrants, the native population gradually adopted the most important neolithic innovations, and farming and cattle-breeding began. In this way, the 'secondary' neolithic civilizations originated, born from the contacts between the newcomers and the descendants of the earlier inhabitants.

In the following pages we will try to give a short description of both the Michelsberg and the funnel-beaker cultures, and to examine the chief characteristics of the 'secondary' neolithic civilizations.

The Michelsberg culture extended over a vast area comprising part of central Germany (upper Weser valley, Saale valley), Bohemia (upper Elbe valley), the valleys of the Rhine, Neckar and Main, Belgium, and further to the south as far as eastern Switzerland, the lake of Constance and the upper Rhine. The most westerly traces are found in Belgium; although it is not represented in the Netherlands, the Michelsberg culture has been found only a few miles from the Dutch border.

The study of the Neolithic in Belgium has been made very difficult because, for a long time, Belgian archaeologists, influenced by the French school, have based their classification of the neolithic civilizations above all, if not exclusively, upon the lithic material, completely neglecting the evidence of the pottery. And, as opposed to the latter, the neolithic stone industry is generally not very typical. They distinguished, apart from the Omalian and the Precampignian (two cultures without polished stone axes), only one single civilization, the so-called 'polished stone axes—neolithic',[1] including not only the Michelsberg culture and the secondary neolithic civilizations, but the late neolithic cultures of the Seine-Oise-Marne and Beaker peoples. Besides, most sites have been excavated in a very inadequate way, and a large part of the material found has either been lost or put in the reserves of a museum, whence it has to be excavated again! It is therefore not very astonishing that only a small number of sites, graves or isolated finds are known which may with some degree of certainty be attributed to the Michelsberg culture. They are scattered all over Belgium, in the provinces of East Flanders (Zwyndrecht), Antwerp (near Antwerp), Limburg (Lommel), Brabant (Ottembourg, Boitsfort), Hainaut (Spiennes, Saint-Symphorien), Namur (Furfooz) and Liège (Avennes). It is very probable that a detailed study of the material kept in the reserves of the museums, will show that a number of sites of the so-called 'polished stone axes—neolithic' do in fact belong to the Michelsberg culture.

The Belgian sites illustrate a number of aspects of the Michelsberg culture, but the information about the way of life of the Michelsberg people, their technical achievements, their houses, etc., is much less complete than in other sites in Switzerland (e.g. Thayngen) and Germany (e.g. Urmitz). The conditions of preservation are much less favourable in our country than in the Swiss lake villages. Some Belgian sites, however, are especially interesting and merit a detailed description.

The site at Boitsfort is on a promontory between two brooks and a series of little lakes, an ideal place for people practising mixed farming, but supplementing their food-supply by hunting and fishing. The rather incomplete excavations have produced no trace of habitations—did these have the same rectangular plan as the wooden houses from Switzerland and Germany?—but quantities of stone artefacts and pottery were discovered. Because of this pottery, mainly tulip-beakers with rounded base, the site can be attributed to the Michelsberg culture. The flint implements were made on the spot, as is shown by the numerous nuclei, the many thousands of flint chippings and the fragments of sandstone 'polissoirs'. The lumps of flint were imported as such, mainly from the mines at Spiennes, to be discussed later. The artefacts include knife-blades, pointed blades, various scrapers, triangular arrow-heads with straight base, tanged and barbed arrow-heads, leaf arrow-heads, and axes, some of which are roughly hewn, others polished. The presence at the base of the promontory, between the two brooks, of what at first sight looks very much like a series of four banks and four ditches, has led some archaeologists to believe that these were fortifications protecting the entrance to the village. Excavations have shown traces of charcoal, fire-reddened earth, flint crackled by action of the heat, flint implements, potsherds and very small fragments of calcined bone. For these reasons, other archaeologists have suggested the presence of cremation burials. In our opinion, both explana-tions must be reconsidered, because recent work at the site has proved that the so-called 'ditches' are the result of the erosion of old trackways. Nothing proves that the bones are human; it seems logical to say that what has been found here are only the traces of hearths. Boitsfort is neither a fortified camp nor a cemetery, but simply a habitation site.

The site of Ottembourg has been explored even less satis-factorily than Boitsfort. There, at the place called Krakelbos, near a habitation site which has yielded stone artefacts and pottery very similar to the objects found at Boitsfort, is situated a rather peculiar monument. It consists of an earthen mound about $4\frac{1}{2}$ ft. high, $42\frac{1}{2}$ ft. wide and 260 ft. long. A few trenches have been dug by earlier explorers, revealing a succession of sand and charcoal layers. These last contained flint implements, fragments of pottery and calcined human bones. The funerary character of this monument seems therefore probable; it is per-haps related to the non-megalithic earthen long barrows of the Windmill Hill culture from southern England. This is, of course, merely a suggestion which can be proved only by systematic excavation. In any case, it must be noted that at Ottembourg the Michelsberg people seem to have practised cremation, while on other sites inhumation was the rule.

Much better investigated and justly famous is the site of Spiennes, which shows a very particular aspect of the Michels-berg culture, namely of an industrial centre where the inhabi-tants had specialized in the exploitation of flint mines. Before describing this site in greater detail, it may be interesting to examine briefly the problem of the beginnings of the mining industry in the Low Countries; because Spiennes is certainly not the only known neolithic centre of this type. In central Belgium, two regions exist where chalk layers of the cretaceous period, containing numerous flint nodules, are found, sometimes near the surface, sometimes deeper: firstly near Mons in Hainaut, secondly in Hesbaye and the Herve area. During the previous periods, the inhabitants of the Low Countries used mainly the flint found on the surface for the manufacture of their implements, or knew only to a very limited extent the industrial potentialities of certain sites (e.g. in mesolithic times at Wommerson). Even the Omalian people did not exploit flint mines. The Precampignian people, on the other hand, were the first to become specialists in the mining of flint in some sites in the north of the Liège province. During the third millennium B.C., a whole series of stations are known where the inhabitants have become specialists in the mining industry: Spiennes, Obourg, Flénu and Strépy in the Mons area, Avennes, Braives and Meffe in Hesbaye, and Rijckholt-Sint-Geertruid in Dutch Limburg, near the Belgian border. The presence of the Michelsberg people has been proved with certainty only at Spiennes and Avennes. However, everywhere else, and even at these two sites, the implements used by the miners show marked influences of the Precampignian stone-industry; certain sites (Obourg, Rijckholt-Sint-Geertruid) have a more archaic aspect than Spiennes, and the Precampignian influence is even more marked. Therefore we suggest that the first miners in the Low Countries were not the Michelsberg people, but the Precampignians and their descendants. These last were, of course, influenced by the mode of life of the Michelsberg people after their arrival here, and their civilization took a pronounced neolithic turn. As regards production, the two most important centres are Rijckholt-Sint-Geertruid (flint objects from these mines have been discovered in the region of Liège, Maaseik, in Belgian Campine and in Dutch

Limburg) and Spiennes (which exported to Flanders, Hainaut, Brabant, Namur and even to Belgian Limburg).

We will describe only Spiennes, where the main mining centre is the 'Camp-à-Cayaux' on the right bank of the River Trouille. The exploitation of the flint-bearing chalk has lasted over a long period, and it is possible to see a certain technical evolution. A start was made in the places where the chalk appeared at or very near the surface; deep pits were dug there or on the slope of the hill by the 'cavage' method (the digging of short horizontal galleries beginning at the slope of the hill). The implements used by the miners during this first phase were still rather primitive, and recall those of Obourg and Rijckholt-Sint-Geertruid. The most typical tool was the Precampignian tranchet; the flint picks, so typical of the next phase, and the polished axes were still scarce. During what might be called the 'classic' Spiennes phase, the deeper chalk layers were exploited. Vertical shafts about 40 in. in diameter and a funnel-like entrance—to prevent the earth from falling in—were sunk to a depth of 40 to over 50 ft. Once the chalk was reached, irregular horizontal galleries were dug radiating in all directions and following the chalk layer. These galleries are very low and the miners had to work in a crouched position. To avoid accidents, pillars of chalk were left standing from place to place. Only the lumps of flint were brought to the surface, while the blocks of chalk were pushed into disused galleries. That mining tragedies already occurred in prehistoric times is shown by the discovery at Obourg of the skeleton of a miner, pick in hand, crushed by the collapsed roof. To dig these shafts and these galleries, the Spiennes miners used deer antler picks and long flint picks with triangular section, of which innumerable specimens have been found. At Spiennes alone many dozens of shafts exist, and it is probable that several of these were being worked at the same time. Sometimes the flint brought to the surface was exported in lumps—as is shown, for example, by the finds at

Plate 14

Boitsfort—but mostly it was worked on the spot. At the Camp-à-Cayaux itself, many flint-working floors have been discovered, established in shallow circular pits about 20 in. deep and 5 ft. in diameter. These pits contain traces of hearths, pottery sherds, implements and the remains of food. Often the mouth of a disused and filled-in vertical shaft has been chosen as the site for one of these working floors. A rather advanced degree of specialization can be seen in these *ateliers*: while in some solely mining picks were made, work in others was confined to splitting the lumps of flint into long blades or making rough axes intended for subsequent polishing. At Spiennes itself polished axes are relatively scarce. It seems that the majority of the axes were only roughed out at the site, to be exported later and polished by their new possessors. At several places in Belgium, sandstone *polissoirs* have been found, either portable or made of solid rocks sticking out of the soil (like the big *polissoirs* at Saint-Mard near Virton (prov. Luxemburg). The Spiennes workmen used antler hammers for the working of the flint. Apart from the tranchets, picks, long blades and axes already mentioned, the stone industry comprised large

Fig. 21

scrapers and very finely retouched leaf arrow-heads. Bone and antler were used for making potter's tools ('*lissoirs*') and wool-carding combs. The most representative selection of Michelsberg pottery has been found at Spiennes. The pots have a smooth surface and are generally plain. But some vases have a lip decorated with fingertip impressions or clay pastilles. Amongst the most typical forms are tulip-beakers with rounded base, spherical flasks with high and almost vertical neck, bowls with flat base and carinated profile, and dishes. Also worthy of mention are the flat discs probably used for the baking of

Plate 13

bread or as covers for containers. No habitation site has yet been discovered at Spiennes. Aerial photography has shown, however, near the Camp-à-Cayaux, the existence of two circular enclosures which might perhaps be interpreted as fortified villages. Only systematic excavations can prove whether this supposition is correct. Not all the inhabitants of Spiennes were miners or flint-workers. Farmers and cattle-breeders must have lived amongst them. In a number of *ateliers* pieces of clay have been found on which the imprint of cereals are still

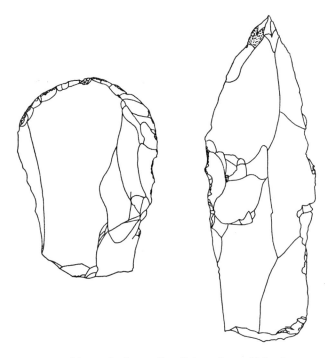

Fig. 21. Implements from Spiennes (prov. Hainaut), 1:2.

visible: millet, spelt, wheat and perhaps oats. The importance of cereals as a food among this people is shown by the presence of grinding stones and baking discs. On the other hand, the food remains have yielded numerous bones of domesticated animals: ox, goat, sheep and pig. Hunting still played a rather important part, as is proved by the presence of the bones of red deer, roe-buck, wild boar and even *bos primigenius*. Several species of snail seem to have been amongst the favourite dishes. Older *ateliers* have sometimes been used as burial places. The Spiennes people seem to have practised the rite of removing the flesh from the bones of their dead, before burying them. In the grave, pottery and tools were deposited; both were sometimes purposely smashed as part of the burial ritual.

This same rite of removing the flesh has also been observed in another Michelsberg site, namely at Furfooz. The 'Trou du Frontal' has been used as an ossuary; the bones of eighteen individuals were discovered there, all mixed together, in a cleft of the rock closed by a dolomite slab. Fifty bones at least show marked traces of cuts made while removing the flesh. Inside this grave were found sherds of a spherical vase of a typical Michelsberg form, with rounded neck, the body of which was decorated with six horizontally perforated knobs.

Traces of simple inhumation were discovered beneath a flint-working floor at Avennes, in a grave containing an adult miner and two children, the skeletons being in correct anatomical relationship. The same is true of the grave at Zwyndrecht, which contained the skeleton of a girl together with a flint blade and a scraper, a tulip-beaker and a vase-support in baked clay. The bronze pin found at the same site by the excavators probably does not come from this grave.

This variety of funerary ritual of the Michelsberg people in Belgium (cremation at Ottembourg, flesh-removal and individual graves at Spiennes, flesh-removal with collective tomb at Furfooz, inhumation at Avennes and Zwyndrecht) is certainly interesting, but has not yet been satisfactorily explained.

The other Belgian sites where traces of the Michelsberg culture have been discovered do not add much to our knowledge of this culture; they are mostly isolated pottery finds: tulip-beakers near Antwerp and at Lommel-Kattenbos, a big carinated bowl with flat base at Saint-Symphorien.

Fig. 22

We agree with E. Vogt, C. J. Becker and Stuart Piggott as to the Eastern origins of the Michelsberg culture and its rela‑ tionship to the Funnel‑beaker culture. It remains true neverthe‑ less that this culture, and more especially its Belgian aspect, shows some affinities with the Windmill Hill culture of southern England, the origins of which must be looked for in the 'western Neolithic', and which is clearly related to the older Cortaillod of Switzerland and the older Chassey of France.

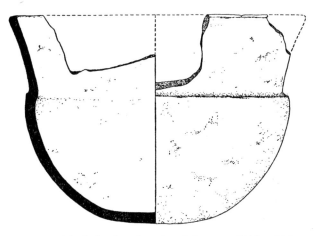

Fig. 22. Tulip‑beaker from the region of Antwerp. Height : $6\frac{3}{8}$ in.

The causeway‑camps call to mind the Urmitz (and perhaps the Spiennes) fortifications; the earthen long barrows make one think of the funeral mound at Ottembourg; the miners of Grimes Graves used tools very similar to the ones of the Belgian neolithic miners; some carinated pots from Sussex and Yorkshire strongly remind one of the tulip‑beakers; lastly, the same wool‑carding combs and leaf arrow‑heads are found in England and Belgium. For these reasons we are ready to admit, with Stuart Piggott, that a group of Michelsberg people did cross the sea and influence the Windmill Hill culture.

F

Radiocarbon readings indicate that the Michelsberg culture started in Western Europe about 2750 B.C. We do not know how long it lasted. During eneolithic times it was replaced in Belgium by the Beaker groups and the Seine-Oise-Marne people. The Beaker people probably arrived in the Low Countries about 2000 B.C., though groups of Michelsberg people may have remained in these regions for some time after this date.

The Funnel-beaker culture spread over a large area to the north of the region occupied by the Michelsberg people, from Poland in the East to the Netherlands in the West, and from southern Norway and central Sweden in the North to Austria in the South. It is only natural that several cultural provinces can be distinguished, each with its own characteristics. The most westerly of these groups includes north-west Germany and the Netherlands. In this last country, the Funnel-beaker culture is almost exclusively represented by graves and isolated pottery finds. A few habitation sites were discovered, but unfortunately destroyed before systematic excavation was possible.

The province of Drenthe is the main centre of this culture; there are to be found nearly all the large megalithic tombs which form the most typical remains of this culture. However, the area covered by the Funnel-beaker people is much larger, and includes other Dutch provinces: Frisia, Groningen, Overijssel, Guelders, North Brabant and Dutch Limburg. The most southerly remains of this culture have been found barely one and a quarter miles from the Belgian frontier; it is therefore quite possible that one day traces of the Funnel-beaker culture will be found somewhere in Belgian Limburg.

It is known that originally the megalithic element formed no part of the Funnel-beaker culture, but came from the megalithic tradition from the West. In Denmark important remains of the pre-megalithic phase of this civilization have been discovered, with a pottery very similar to the Michelsberg pottery. These have been dated to about 2700–2500 B.C. (phases A and B of the Scandinavian Early Neolithic). It is conceivable that a similar pre-megalithic phase existed in the Netherlands, but this remains rather uncertain: only a single piece of pottery from the Enschede Museum may point in this direction. Be this as it may, from the next phase onward (Scandinavian Early Neolithic C, about 2500–2200 B.C.), the Funnel-beaker culture flourished very strongly in the Netherlands. Several types of tombs can be distinguished. They fall into two categories: the big collective megalithic tombs (of at least five different types) and the individual graves (which can either be stone cists, or simple inhumations in flat graves). The megalithic tombs (*hunebedden*) are all, apart from a fragmentary specimen in the province of Groningen, and two destroyed monuments in the provinces of Overijssel and Frisia, concentrated in Drenthe, where even now fifty-four of them can be seen, and where the sites of about thirty others are known, destroyed during recent centuries. In fact, they are limited to the region of the glacial moraines. Outside this area, the Funnel-beaker people buried their dead in simple inhumation graves, because they did not have the big boulders of various shapes necessary for the construction of the megalithic monuments. All the *hunebedden* have certain characteristics in common. The burial chambers are rectangular rooms partially dug into the soil, and varying between 11 and over 65 ft. in length. The walls are made of two parallel rows of orthostats, every pair supporting a single cap-stone and thus forming a series of trilithons placed one next to the other. The short sides are closed by one or two orthostats. The burial chamber is hermetically sealed by closing the interstices between orthostats and horizontal slabs with stones and rubble. The floor is usually made of large pebbles covered with gravel. The bodies and the grave-goods—mainly pottery—

Plate 16

Fig. 23

were deposited on this floor, sometimes in several layers separated by a secondary pavement. A circular or oval mound
covered, either completely or partially, these funeral chambers,
which usually faced East–West. In some cases the grave mound
reached only as high as the top of the orthostats, thus leaving
the cap-stones visible. The base of the mound was composed
of stones to strengthen the orthostats, while the upper part consisted of sand. In some of these monuments, as in Germany and
in Scandinavia, it has been established that the body of the
mound contained broken flint tools (ritual?) and numerous
pottery sherds deposited in front of the outer entrance, where
they seem to have been put on purpose, which might mean that
certain ritual activities accompanied the building of the grave
mound. The difference between the several types of *hunebedden*
can best be seen in the entrances. Usually, the entrance is
situated in the middle of one of the long sides, the one looking
to the south. One, or occasionally two stones or 'doorsteps'
mark the entrance to the grave itself. In a few monuments the
entrance consists of a passage, made of one or two pairs of orthostats supporting a single horizontal cap-stone; this passage has
the same type of floor as the grave-chamber itself. They are true
passage-graves. A good example is the *hunebed* D 53 at Havelte.
The entrance to the passage is continued in a circle of uprights
around the base of the mound. In the Netherlands such a stone
circle is found only around the passage-graves. In other cases,
as in tomb D 18 at Buinen, the entrance is shaped like a porch.
Sometimes it is formed only by a more pronounced widening
between two orthostats of the south wall: this is the case with
tomb D 25 at Bronnegger. Lastly, in one case—tomb D 41 at
Emmen—there is no visible entrance and the tomb is closed on
all four sides. Tomb D 43 on the Schimmeres at Emmen is
also unique in the Netherlands; this monument, the largest
Dutch megalithic tomb, consists of two funeral chambers
originally enclosed within the same mound, the base of which

Fig. 23a

Fig. 23b

Fig. 23c
Fig. 23d
Fig. 23e

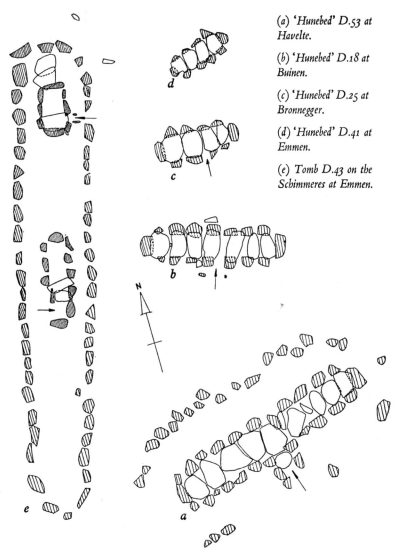

(a) 'Hunebed' D.53 at Havelte.

(b) 'Hunebed' D.18 at Buinen.

(c) 'Hunebed' D.25 at Bronnegger.

(d) 'Hunebed' D.41 at Emmen.

(e) Tomb D.43 on the Schimmeres at Emmen.

Fig. 23. Plan of several 'hunebedden' of the province Drenthe.

b 50 ft. long, others to scale.

was surrounded by a kind of rectangular wall, formed of big uprights placed side by side, the interstices being filled in with small stones. Of the individual graves, mention must be made of a few stone cists (Diever, Eext, Zeijen) which are almost like miniature megalithic tombs (the one at Diever measures 11 ft. 9¾ in. by 2 ft. 7½ in., the one at Zeijen 9 ft. 10 in. by 2 ft.). The walls are formed by uprights, but no horizontal slabs exist. These were probably replaced by a roofing in wood. The floor is made of large pebbles. The base of the cist was surrounded with small stones and the whole structure was covered with a mound, in which secondary graves were dug in different periods (from Neolithic to Iron Age). Lastly, at several places in the provinces of Drenthe (Zuidwolde, Sleen), Guelders (Lake Uddel, near Apeldoorn) and Overijssel (Ambt-Hardenberg), ordinary flat graves have been discovered in which the grave-goods were deposited next to the dead. Some of these graves were simply rectangular pits, in others the body was protected by a few stones placed around it.

Recent work by L. Kaelas, based upon the study of the pottery of the Dutch Funnel-beaker culture, has shown that, contrary to the generally accepted theory, the different types of collective tombs together with the individual inhumations go back to phase C of the Scandinavian Early Neolithic (2500–2200 B.C.). The stone cists, too, are very old and start at least in the Middle Neolithic I (about 2200–2100 B.C.), if not already in the Early Neolithic C. This point is extremely important, because it proves that the passage-graves of the Dutch and north-west German Funnel-beaker group are older than their Scandinavian equivalents, which makes it necessary to reconsider the problem of how this type of grave reached Scandinavia, where it is so characteristic of the Middle Neolithic.

The pottery, tools, weapons and ornaments of the Dutch Funnel-beaker people are known almost exclusively from the grave-goods. They were placed in the funerary chambers and the entrances of the *hunebedden*. It is quite possible that numerous potsherds, probably remains of ritual activities may still be recovered from the area in front of the tomb, as has been shown by finds in Scandinavia and Germany. The shapes of the pot⁄tery are very varied: typical funnel⁄beakers (from which the name of the culture is derived), small collared flasks, buckets with oblique sides, carinated pots with vertical neck and handle, bowls with rounded base, bowls with a low foot, dishes, etc. The decoration consists of deep vertical and hori⁄zontal grooves, chevrons and triangles which are very well adapted to the shape of the pot and accentuate its different elements. These designs have been impressed in the clay either by a little wooden stick or a bone point, or by a twig fitted with a thread⁄wound stamp, or else by a toothed stick the im⁄pression of which imitated the above⁄mentioned technique. Afterwards the grooves were filled in with a white paste. The ornamental motifs include the so⁄called 'double eye', borrowed from the Western megalithic world and having a religious significance, probably connected with the solar cult. There is a notable absence, in the Netherlands, of the cult⁄bowls on a high foot and the flat discs with hollowed⁄out handle (sun⁄idols?) that are so characteristic of the Scandinavian Funnel⁄beaker group. The only high⁄footed bowl, found in the *hunebed* at Drouwen, is of a completely different type and is probably an imported piece from the Jordansmühl culture (Silesia). Two different stylistic groups can be distinguished in the pottery: one (Drouwen style) with more angular shapes, the other (Havelte style) characterized by more rounded forms. Both styles are also found in north⁄west Germany. One may be earlier than the other, but the possibility is not ruled out that both may belong to the same period, though representing dif⁄ferent traditions.

A few archaic axes and scrapers of northern mesolithic tradi⁄tion do still appear in the lithic industry. More typical of the

Plates 18–22

Funnel-beaker culture are polished thin-butted axes and trans-verse arrow-heads. The personal ornaments include amber beads from Denmark and jet beads from England. In two megalithic tombs metal objects have been found: a few bronze fragments in *hunebed* D 19 at Drouwen, and two copper spirals in the primary level in *hunebed* D 28 at Buinen. Very probably these ornaments were imported from Silesia (Jordansmühl culture), like the high-foot bowl from Drouwen. The presence of these objects shows that trade relations existed between the Dutch Funnel-beaker people and the British Isles on the one hand, and the East and the North on the other.

Plate 23

No habitation site of this culture has been excavated in the Netherlands. We can visualize the daily life of its people, how-ever, through the work done at the site of Dümmerlohausen in Oldenburg (Germany), where a complete village of this cul-ture has been systematically studied. This village, situated near a lake-shore, was protected by a multiple palisade. The forty-odd houses were rectangular in plan (13–16 ft. long by 20–23 ft. wide) and consisted generally of two rooms preceded by a porch. The walls were made of wooden posts with wattle-and-daub, the floor being made of boards. The inhabitants prac-tised mixed farming; they knew *triticum monococcum,* spelt, wheat, barley, apple, hazel, raspberry and elder. Cattle, sheep, pig and dog are amongst the domesticated animals. It is not certain that the numerous horse-bones found there belong to domesticated animals. Hunting and fishing complemented the food-stuffs, the game including otter, beaver, red deer, elk, roe-deer, wild boar, fox, wolf, bear and wild cattle.

In the Netherlands, the Funnel-beaker culture began about the middle of the third millennium B.C.; it lasted for quite a long time,[2] its last phase being contemporaneous with the early beakers with protruding foot—starting at about 2000 B.C.—of whom more will be said in the next chapter. In a few megalithic tombs sherds of late specimens of the Corded-ware group and of early bell-beakers have been found. The floor of some barrows of the Beaker culture contained 'megalithic' pottery, thus giving a solid *terminus post quem*. It would seem that the Funnel-beaker culture lasted till about 1800 B.C.

It must also be borne in mind that, at one time, a group of Dutch Funnel-beaker people may have emigrated to England. Indeed, the megalithic tombs of the Medway valley (Kent) present certain analogies with the Dutch ones. No definite statement about this can be given, however, before the systematic excavation of one of these English tombs.

The neolithic civilizations certainly influenced the older native populations of the Low Countries. Some of these groups seem only to have adopted certain technical innovations, like the use of polished axes; others, on the contrary, completely changed their way of life and became farmers and cattle-breeders.

Stray finds of polished axes have been reported from the whole territory of Belgium and the Netherlands. A typological study of the Dutch axes has shown that, north of a line going from the Zuider Zee to the German border, through the province of Overijssel, axes of Nordic type are found almost exclusively: thin-butted axes with rectangular section and thick-butted axes. South of this line, on the other hand, the axes are mainly of the Western type: thin-butted axes with oval section. No such study has been made of the Belgian material, but it seems that almost all polished axes are of the Western type. It must be pointed out, however, that these axes belong not only to the Neolithic, but have been used during the whole of the late Neolithic Period and even the Bronze Age.

Amongst the groups still adhering to the mesolithic way of life were the Tardenoisians, established in a few sandy areas like the Belgian Campine and North Brabant in the Netherlands. On numerous sites polished axes and microliths have been found together. We have already mentioned that in the upper level at Zonhoven, microliths have been found made of fragments of polished axes.

Groups with Campignian traditions are known from other regions. The numerous flint-mining sites have already been described. Others, with tranchets and transverse arrow-heads, come from the north of the Liège province, Brabant (e.g. Genval), and the hills of South Flanders (Kemmelberg, Rode Berg, Scherpenberg).

In neolithic times, the marshy region of the Scheldt and its tributaries (Flanders) was rather densely populated. Man lived on the highest points (e.g. Mendonk) or in lake dwellings. A few are known from the Scheldt valley itself (Melle, Oude-naarde), from the River Lys (Afsne) and from the River Mandel (Dentergem, Emelgem, Roulers). None of these villages has been satisfactorily excavated, and we know almost nothing of their appearance. Pointed stakes were driven vertically through the marshy soil into the earth; they were joined by transverse beams. The houses were then built on these foundations. The villages were inhabited for a very long period, some even as late as the Middle Ages. Because during the excavations no attention was paid to stratigraphy, objects of widely different periods have become mixed. The best-known site is Dentergem, where two habitations have been recognized, one occupied from the Neolithic until the final Bronze Age, the other from the Iron Age until the Middle Ages. Neolithic implements include blades, scrapers, tranchets, polished axes, arrow-heads of Spiennes and Obourg flint; antler hoes, tool-handles and hammers of the same material were also found. Agriculture is proved by the presence of grinding stones and calcined grain, cattle-breeding by the bones of cattle, sheep, goat and pig.

The neolithic remains are very scarce in the densely wooded Ardennes region. The Meuse valley, on the other hand, seems to have been more thickly populated. A few habitation sites have been discovered on promontories delimited on three sides by steep cliffs, and easily defensible by a palisade on the fourth side: these are the so-called promontory forts ('*éperons barrés*'), where later the Iron Age *oppida* were generally established. It is not certain, however, that already in neolithic times artificial defences completed the natural ones. Amongst the sites already occupied in neolithic times are the Hastedon plateau at Saint-Servais near Namur, the Camp de Bonne near Modave, Til-Château at Hotton and Insemont near Hastière. Numerous microliths of Tardenoisian tradition have been found there, together with polished axes, scrapers, piercers, blades and arrow-heads of different types (triangular, tanged and with transver-sal cutting edge). The most characteristic relics of this Meuse Neolithic, however, are the funerary caves. The same caves which had been used in palaeolithic times for habitation, now served as tombs for the neolithic people. Most of these caves are collective burials, but the funeral rites are varied. Sometimes the dead were buried side by side and the skeletons have been found in proper anatomical relationship; or at every new in-humation, the old bones were thrown on a heap at the back of the cave, though the skulls were neatly placed in a row; some-times too, as in the Trou du Frontal at Furfooz already mentioned, flesh-removal was practised. The skeletal remains show that the inhabitants of the Meuse area belonged to very different physical types. On a few skulls traces of trepanation can be seen. This operation was sometimes performed *in vivo,* and in some cases the patient even seems to have survived, which is rather remarkable considering the very primitive in-struments then in use. Sometimes trepanation was practised *post mortem,* probably for a magical purpose: the cut-out bone discs were worn as amulets. A few flint artefacts and sometimes a few pottery sherds make up the contents of these funerary caves. Unfortunately, this pottery has often been neglected and inadequately studied. Otherwise it might perhaps have been possible to attribute these graves to a better-known neolithic culture. It was by this means that the grave from the Trou du Frontal, at Furfooz, was shown to belong to the Michelsberg culture. Quite a few of these caves may have been used as burial places either by the Michelsberg, or by the Seine-Oise-Marne people of late neolithic times. The rite of *post mortem* trepanation, of which traces have been found in these caves, and which was also performed by the SOM people, points in this direction, but only detailed study can confirm this hypothesis. These caves are to be found all along the valley of the Meuse and its tributaries, but most of them are concentrated in the south of the province of Namur (Hastière, Maurenne, Onhaye, Anthée, Blaimont, Gendron, Furfooz with five caves). Others have been discovered at Huccorgne (prov. Liège), Sclaigneaux (prov. Namur), Hotton (prov. Luxemburg), etc. Only one cave is known which was still in use as a habitation site in neolithic times: the exit of the famous caves at Han, which was inhabited during the whole of the Neolithic Period and the Bronze Age. The neolithic level has yielded a magnificent necklace made of about 300 perforated teeth of wolf, dog, fox, beaver, horse, ox, wild boar and bear.

In the Netherlands, 95% of the remains of neolithic times have been found in the eastern provinces and belong to the Danubian, the Funnel-beaker and the late neolithic Beaker cultures. This is readily explained by the fact that during the Atlantic phase the western part of the Netherlands was completely transformed into a marshy, inhospitable region. However, the few traces of neolithic civilization found there are not without interest. Two habitation sites of an as yet unsatisfactorily known secondary neolithic culture must be mentioned: one at Zandwerven (North Holland), the other at Hekelingen (to the west of Rotterdam, prov. South Holland). Cattle-breeding was not unknown to these people, though they lived mainly from fishing (sturgeon bones have been found), mussel, fishing and hunting (bones from red deer, roe,deer, wild cattle, wild boar, beaver and otter). A few post,holes from Heke, lingen suggest rectangular houses. The stone industry includes thin,butted polished axes with oval section, some of which, having been broken, had been re,utilized to make smaller tools, piercers, scrapers and petit,tranchet arrow,heads. A few bone points and antler tool,handles have also been found. The pottery sherds are not very numerous and it has not been pos, sible to reconstruct even a single vessel. The clay is stone, gritted; the surface is smooth. The pots have a flat base; the sides are generally plain and only a few sherds show rows of stick,impressions. Sometimes, a row of little holes is made under the lip. All this is not very typical, because the same characteristics have been found in quite a number of neolithic cultures. Up to now it has not been possible to include the Zandwerven and Hekelingen people in a wider cultural relationship.

No direct traces have yet been discovered of the nordic secondary neolithic, the so,called 'pitted,ware' group. It is conceivable, however, that these may appear as a result of new excavations or of a re,study of museum and private collections. Indeed, in the Netherlands this culture has almost certainly influenced the evolution of the Beaker civilization, to be dis, cussed in the next chapter. The Netherlands may therefore be regarded as probably belonging to the area of distribution of this Nordic secondary Neolithic.

CHAPTER VI

Late Neolithic Migrations

A NEW SUCCESSION of migrations and invasions marked the centuries which, in Western Europe, formed the transition between the Neolithic and the Bronze Age. Unlike the earlier migrations of neolithic farmers, they did not always have a peaceful character. Their origin and development fall outside the scope of this book, and we must confine ourselves to discussing their repercussions in the Low Countries. Again a clear distinction must be made between conditions in the North and in the South. While in the Netherlands and in the northern provinces of Belgium traces have been found of the Beaker peoples, southern Belgium (the Meuse valley and the area situated to the south-east of this river) was invaded by the so-called Seine-Oise-Marne (SOM) culture. Each will be described in turn.

Until recently it has generally been admitted that the Beaker civilization appeared in our regions only after its separate elements (Corded-ware and Bell-beaker cultures) had become amalgamated into one single civilization. However, recent work done on the pottery, together with a number of radio-carbon readings, has shown that these two main elements reached the Low Countries separately with an interval of one or two centuries between them, finally to become one culture after having incorporated certain neolithic elements found here.

The Corded-ware culture as well as the Bell-beaker culture is characterized by individual burial-mounds and flat graves, in contrast with the collective megalithic tombs of the Funnel-beaker people already mentioned and of the SOM civilization which will be described later. These tombs and the grave-goods are indeed almost the only source of information we have: only a few inadequately known habitation sites and many surface finds may be added. A few isolated finds in Belgium can tell us something about the area of distribution of the Beaker cul⁄tures, but for all other information we must turn to excavations in the Netherlands.

The study of the late neolithic barrows was begun in the Netherlands by Holwerda, and continued by van Giffen and the archaeologists of his school, using a very refined technique, the so⁄called 'quadrant method'. The internal structure of these burials has in this way been very satisfactorily studied. Unfor⁄tunately quite a lot of these tumuli had already been pillaged by amateur 'archaeologists', while many of the most characteristic vessels come from earlier excavations. Thus, though we know a lot about the structure of the barrows on one hand, and of the grave⁄goods on the other, our knowledge of the relationship between the different types of beakers and the types of grave monuments is still inadequate.

Let us begin with a short description of the tombs. The dead are always inhumed, lying on their side in a crouched position, either in a grave⁄pit or on ground level, the grave⁄goods being deposited next to the body. In some cases a light wooden con⁄struction was erected over the grave. This was either cone⁄shaped, but with a quadrangular plan and an entrance (in a barrow at Eext (Drenthe) it measures 4 ft. 7 in. by 5 ft. 3 in.), or beehive⁄shaped (diameter 4 ft. 7 in./5 ft. 7 in.; height up to 5 ft. 7 in.). In this last case, the body is either lying on its side, or buried in a crouched sitting position. On top of all this (grave plus hut or beehive) a mound of sand of varying dimen⁄sions was raised. In a number of instances the grave itself was closely surrounded by a narrow circular foundation trench in which traces of closely spaced stakes can be seen. This palisade is sometimes replaced by a circle of widely spaced posts. In other cases, excavation has revealed inside the core of the mound

Plate 17

Fig. 24

95

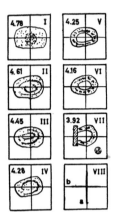

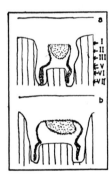

Fig. 24. Plan of a bee-hive-tomb from Onnen (prov. Groningen).

Plate 15

either a stone revetment or a circle of closely packed small stones. Lastly, the base of the tumulus may be surrounded by one or two concentric ditches. All these structural elements occur in different combinations, so that scarcely ever are two absolutely identical barrows found. Simple burial-mounds do not occur very frequently: sometimes traces of one or two vertical posts can be seen at the centre, near the grave; at other times, no internal structure whatsoever exists. In adjacent countries where the Beaker civilizations are represented, the excavations have been less satisfactorily carried out. It is therefore difficult to determine whether all structural elements found in the Dutch barrows derive from these civilizations or represent adaptations of elements borrowed from older cultures. It is possible that the palisade and the circle of posts are only a transposition in wood of the orthostat circle surrounding the base of the megalithic passage-graves; they may have the same ritual or magical significance. It is also conceivable that the stone revetments sometimes found inside the barrows are derived from the Funnel-beaker culture. Indeed, during several centuries the representatives of the latter lived side by side with the Beaker people and many cultural contacts between the two were established, about which more will be said later.

A typical example of the complexity of the structural elements found in these barrows is given by tumulus III at Zeijen (Drenthe). The body was buried in a grave-pit; the grave-goods consisted of two beakers with herring-bone pattern. A beehive construction of about $6\frac{1}{2}$ ft. in diameter was raised above the burial. Traces of a post-circle $24\frac{1}{2}$ ft. in diameter were discovered inside the mound itself, while around the base of the barrow ran a ditch 33 ft. in diameter. Similar examples are to be found in other places, for instance in the 'Eppies bergje' (at Odoorn, Drenthe), where the grave-pit was surrounded by a narrow circular foundation trench, a stone revetment and a deep peripheral ditch.

It must also be mentioned that ordinary inhumation, in flat graves, without barrow or internal grave structure, was also practised by the Beaker people. Examples have been found at Sleen and at Vredenheim (Drenthe).

As mentioned earlier, it is the pottery which makes it possible to distinguish between the two main elements of the Beaker civilizations. This pottery can be separated into two groups.

The first group represents the tradition of the Corded-ware culture. It is characterized by slender, S-profiled vessels, the foot being small, but distinctly protruding; the ornamentation is limited to the upper part, between the rim and the greatest width. The evolution of this type of beaker can be followed by means of the typology of the decoration and the shape of the foot; it is confirmed by radiocarbon datings. In the older types, the decoration consists of a series of cord-impressed horizontal lines circling the pot. These cord-impressed grooves—which may be replaced by non-corded lines—sometimes alternate with zones of oblique 'herring-bone' pattern executed with a plain implement or spatula. Later, the decoration consists of alternately hatched zones bordered by grooves. Then comes a 'herring-bone' decoration without separating grooves, while on the even more recent beakers zones hatched in one direction only, with or without separating grooves, can be seen. A few plain beakers have also been found. Plates 29, 30

This pottery is closely related to the *Westdeutsche Becher-gruppe*-ware, itself deriving from the Saxo-Thuringian *Schnur-keramik*. The earlier beaker-types are still very much like the ones found in western and central Germany, while the later ones are local evolutions. The objects associated in closed finds with the beakers of this first group include knives consisting of a long unretouched flint flake, small polished axes made of flint or hard rock, a few battle-axes and sometimes a second vessel, generally smaller and undecorated. Of the large amphorae,

Plate 31

frequently associated with the Saxo-Thuringian corded beakers, only five examples are known from the Netherlands. To the same culture also belong big coarse beakers with 'short-wave moulding', and with sometimes a wavy relief cordon below the rim. These were probably used as storage jars. On the other hand, no stone wrist-guards have been found in these ensembles, nor flint arrow-heads, Grand Pressigny flint blades, amber beads, V-perforated amber buttons or metal objects, all of which exist in association with beakers of the second group.

The barrows of this first group sometimes contain a central beehive structure, often an intermediate circular foundation trench, and are frequently surrounded by a peripheral ditch. Only one habitation site of this group is known, at Zandwerven (northern Holland), where the upper level has yielded pottery useful for dating the older phases of this civilization. The lower level belongs to a secondary neolithic culture which has been described in the preceding chapter. This site does not teach us much about the way of life of the Beaker people, but it may be supposed that they were mainly occupied with stock-raising and, in a lesser degree, with agriculture, like their kinsmen from western and central Germany and from the Danish *Enkeltgravkultur,* as is indicated by grain-impressions on some beakers.

It may incidentally be mentioned that the introduction of the ard in the Low Countries dates from the Beaker civilizations, or a little before, since traces of furrows made by this primitive plough were discovered under a Beaker barrow, at Gasteren (Drenthe). It remains an open question whether this imple-ment was introduced here by the Beaker people, or by their predecessors, the Funnel-beaker people.

Recent radiocarbon readings place the arrival in the Nether-lands of elements from the *Westdeutsche Bechergruppe* in the last centuries of the third millennium, between 2200 and 2000 B.C., the later pottery-types of this group bringing us near 1600 B.C.

On their arrival, these newcomers established themselves in a few regions only, mainly in the north and south of the Veluwe and at the western limit of the sandy areas in the north of the Netherlands; in the other regions only a few traces of this first phase can be found. It should be noted that at the beginning, they carefully avoided the most important area of the Funnel-beaker settlement (Drenthe). Later, however, they did enter this region and made contact with the people of the megalithic tombs, as is shown not only by late beaker-sherds found inside several *hunebedden,* but also by hybrid forms of the pottery and its decoration. They also spread out into other areas, to northern Holland, Guelders, Overijssel—where their evolution had a rather special character, about which more will be said later—and to central Dutch Limburg. In Belgium fragments of only one single rather late type of beaker of this group have been dis-covered, namely at Overpelt (Limburg).

The second element of the Beaker civilizations belongs to the western group of the bell-beakers. It seems to have reached the Low Countries by two separate ways. The first, the sea route, started from Brittany and reached on the one hand the Temse and Termonde area in Belgium by way of the River Scheldt, and on the other, following the coast, the northern provinces of the Netherlands. The second reached Belgian and Dutch Limburg, the Veluwe and Drenthe by land, following the Rhine.

The beakers of this second group have a comparatively broad flat base without protruding foot and with ornamentation that is not restricted to the upper part. They are generally rather wide (the width often exceeding the height), but more slender types also occur. They have either an S-shaped or a carinated profile with sometimes a clear and angular separation between neck and body. The surface is covered with a slip and is smoothly burnished. The decoration, in horizontal zones, is applied with a toothed spatula (*gradine*).

The Bell-beaker people arrived in the Low Countries around 2000 B.C. In contrast to the first group, they almost immediately moved into the area occupied by the megalithic tomb people, with whom they had frequent peaceful contacts. Their earliest beakers, still of a 'pan-european' type, are almost as wide as they are high; they have an S-profile and are decorated with alternate plain and *gradine*-applied ornamental horizontal zones, each zone (decorated and undecorated) being of equal width. These older-type beakers occur in Belgium in the Temse-Termonde region, and in the Netherlands mainly in Drenthe, but also in the west of Guelders and the east of Overijssel and Frisia. A slow evolution of these beakers can be seen: the ornamental zones are more contracted, the undecorated ones wider. Only three decorated bands subsist, one on the neck, one at the greatest width, one immediately above the base. The beakers become bigger and wider. These pots of a more evolved type are found in Drenthe, in the Veluwe and in Dutch Limburg. Lastly, in the final stage of this evolution— between 1800 and 1500 B.C.—the Veluwe beakers occur (Abercromby's 'Batavian' type). Here, the transition between neck and shoulder is clearly angular; their width is greater than the height, and sometimes the neck is cylindrical. The decoration is rich and varied; undecorated zones have practically disappeared. Vertical hatching, cross-hatching and zigzag lines exist; the shoulder is decorated with a continuous frieze of triangles or metopes. Some of these elements, like the metopes, also occur on bell-beakers from central Germany and Bohemia. It may well be that at this time new elements from the Bell-beaker people, coming from these regions, reinforced the already established colonies in the Netherlands. The Veluwe beakers are very numerous (no less than eighty complete ones are known, with fragments of hundreds of others); by far the most have been found in the Veluwe; a few come from Drenthe and the Nijmegen and Hilversum regions.

Fig. 25

Plate 28

Plate 27

Chronologically parallel with this first group of bell-beakers, a second group exists, but with a different evolution: bell-beakers that have borrowed the ornamentation of the beakers with protruding foot. They are generally slender, with S-shaped or carinated profile. A first group combines the alternate oblique hatchings, applied with a toothed spatula, with the cord-impressions: it occurs on the Veluwe, in Dutch Limburg and in the Belgian Campine (prov. of Limburg

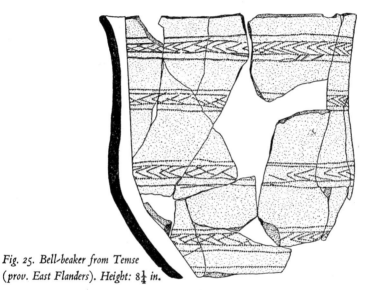

Fig. 25. Bell-beaker from Temse (prov. East Flanders). Height: 8¼ in.

and Antwerp). A second group is decorated with cord-impressions covering the whole beaker; more numerous than the first group, it is found rarely in Drenthe, Overijssel, the Veluwe and again mainly in Dutch and Belgian Limburg. Lastly, less frequently found, are bell-beakers decorated in zones, but with a plain spatula. Thus, in these three types of bell-beakers clear influences of the Corded-ware civilization are to be seen. The principal area of contact between both groups seems to have been Dutch Limburg.

The closed finds with bell-beakers contain copper tanged knife-daggers, stone wrist-guards, triangular flint arrow-heads mostly tanged and barbed, battle-axes, Grand Pressigny daggers, amber beads and pendants, V-perforated amber buttons, and sometimes a gold ornament. The richest associations belong to the period of the arrival of the Bell-beaker people. The Odoorn barrow (Drenthe) contained a beaker of pan-European type, a copper dagger, a copper awl, a spiral bracelet made of thick copper wire, two amber beads and two tiny rectangular strips of sheet gold, the ends bent over to penannular form and perforated. This find illustrates the trade relations that existed between the Netherlands and the North and South along the Atlantic shores: the gold ornaments and the beaker itself probably are of Breton origin, the amber pearls coming from the Baltic.[1]

It is almost impossible to attribute a definite barrow type to the Bell-beaker culture. The body was deposited in a shallow grave or on the surface, and covered by a mound of sand. Generally speaking, no central structure exists (though the Odoorn barrow may have had a beehive construction); occasionally an intermediate or peripheral palisade occurs; peripheral ditches are frequent. Flat inhumation graves were not unknown to the Bell-beaker people.

During the first centuries of the second millennium, a group of Bell-beaker people coming from the delta-area of the big rivers arrived in Great Britain, where they introduced the bell-beakers with contracted zone-decoration, the beakers with over-all decoration of cord-impressed lines and the big pot-beakers about which more will be said presently.

The two Beaker civilizations which have been discussed, arrived separately in the Low Countries; there they influenced each other and came in contact with the older neolithic cultures already established in our regions, e.g. the Funnel-beaker people and the Pitted-ware culture. We have already described

Fig. 26a. Section of the copper dagger from the Odoorn barrow. (Fig. 26c). 2:3.

the group of bell-beakers with decoration borrowed from corded-ware. On the other hand, in the corded-ware group a series of hybrid forms due to bell-beaker influences can also be seen: in Limburg some beakers with protruding foot have a decoration extending lower than the widest part of the vessel; in Drenthe and the Veluwe some have a vertical herring-bone ornamentation, others have been decorated by the *gradine*

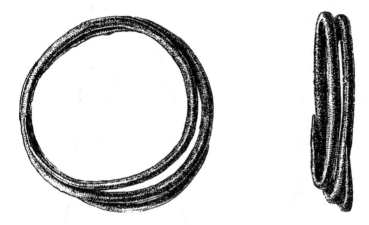

Fig. 26b. Spiral bracelet from the Odoorn barrow. 2:3.

technique or present a zig-zag pattern. Most of these hybrid forms seem to be rather late.

Contact with the people of the megalithic tombs is evidenced not only by the presence in a few *hunebedden* of bell-beakers and late corded-ware, but also by a group of beakers decorated with thread-wound impressions, a technique borrowed from the megalithic tomb civilization. These rather hybrid beakers are found mainly in the east of the province of Overijssel (and also across the frontier in Germany) and in Guelders; a few isolated finds are reported from other regions, e.g. in Drenthe. Only one beaker of this type has been discovered in Belgium (Lana-ken, prov. Limburg). It seems that, chronologically, these

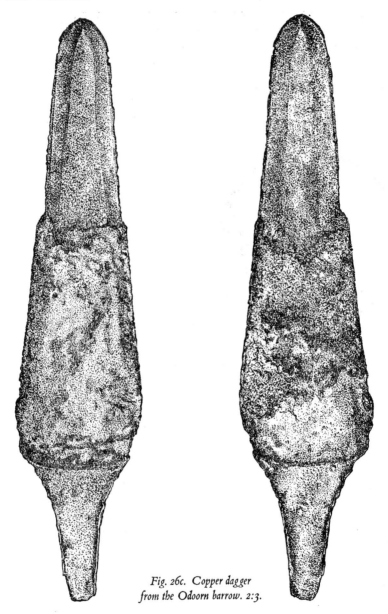

Fig. 26c. Copper dagger from the Odoorn barrow. 2:3.

beakers can be placed between 1900 B.C. and the end of the late Neolithic Period. As is apparent from their shape and decoration, some of these vessels seem to go back to the traditions of the corded-ware group (protruding foot, ornamentation limited to the upper part of the vase); others show similarities with the bell-beakers (no foot, zonal or over-all decoration, decoration on the inside of the rim, zig-zag ornamentation). Some even seem to have been influenced by the pitted-ware pottery (row of small perforations under the rim, very narrow base, large vessels).

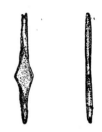

Fig. 26d. Copper awl from the Odoorn barrow. 2:3.

A last category of vessels which have been connected with the Beaker civilizations are the 'pot-beakers': giant vessels, very coarsely fashioned, with rounded or very narrow base, often rusticated or decorated all over with finger-tip ornamentation or nail impressions. Some have a row of little holes under the rim. These pots have probably no funerary significance, but have been explained as storage jars (?), frequently found in habitation sites. These pot-beakers, related to the *Riesenbecher* of north-western Germany, are very probably derived from the pottery of the nordic 'dwelling-place' or 'pitted-ware' culture. Their area of distribution coincides, in the Low Countries, with the area of distribution of the Beaker civilizations.[2] For this reason, numerous archaeologists concede that the pot-beakers are nothing but the vessels for everyday use of the Beaker people. That contacts between the beakers and the pot-beakers existed seems undeniable: the ornamentation of some pot-beakers is very similar to that of the Veluwe beakers. It is also reasonably certain that the Bell-beaker people, coming from the Netherlands, introduced the big coarse urns into Great Britain, e.g. in the Cambridge region and at Woodhenge, where they have even been used during part of the Bronze Age. However, the origins of pot-beakers and beakers are completely different. We therefore suggest that these pots belong to a secondary neolithic culture, related to the Nordic

Plate 26

Fig. 26e. Gold ornaments and amber beads from the Odoorn barrow. 2:3.

Grubekeramiske kultur, which established rather close contacts with the Beaker civilizations.

Before leaving the Netherlands, the discovery in Drenthe of timber trackways through marshy areas (Buinen, Valthe) must be mentioned, which pollen-analysis has dated in the late Neolithic Period.

Plate 25

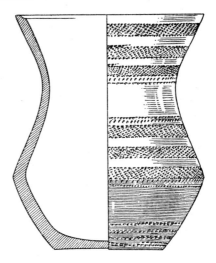

Fig. 26f. Beaker from the Odoorn barrow. Height 7⅛ in.

At about the same time that the Netherlands and northern Belgium saw the arrival and the establishment of elements belonging to the Beaker people, another invasion took place in south Belgium, and more particularly in the province of Hainaut, the valley of the Meuse and the Famenne: the so-called Seine-Oise-Marne (SOM) invasions from the South. This is a secondary neolithic culture from the region north of the Seine, between the Oise and the Marne, derived from a native mesolithic culture which had first been influenced by the western Neolithic (Camp-de-Chassey and Fort-Harrouard) and later by the megalithic traditions from southern

France (Arles) and Brittany. In an older, pre-megalithic phase, elements from the SOM people emigrated to western Switzer-land, where they introduced the so-called Horgen culture; during a more recent period, other elements of this people, whose warrior-like character has often been emphasized, pushed to the North, through Belgium along the Meuse valley and the Famenne depression, to reach the Rhine, the valley of the Lippe and finally western and central Sweden. The traces left by this SOM invasion in Belgium are not very numerous, and it is not possible to determine the duration of the SOM occupa-tion of our regions.[3]

Apart from a few isolated finds, the SOM civilization is represented in Belgium only by graves and—perhaps—by a series of menhirs. From the Netherlands we know only a habitation site. In France, the SOM people buried their dead in collective tombs, either in artificial caves dug into the chalk of the Champagne, or in megalithic gallery-graves. Natural caves as well as megalithic tombs were used as ossuaries in Belgium. In this country, intensive agriculture must have destroyed a number of megalithic monuments; only two still exist, though the sites of two others, destroyed during the last century, are known. The two still visible are situated at Wéris (in the north of the province of Luxembourg). The smallest is a dug-out gallery-grave; the walls of the funerary chamber (length 15 ft. 1 in., width 3 ft. 11 in., height 2 ft.) are made of orthostats in pudding-stone, the roof being composed of three massive horizontal slabs. In front of this chamber was a paved ante-chamber, surrounded by orthostats, two of which still exist; both chambers are separated by a transverse slab, pierced by a door-shaped hole. The interstices between the orthostats were filled in with loose stones. In the grave-chamber were found traces of a ritual funeral meal (charcoal from a hearth and several animal bones) and the bones of several individuals, together with flint implements (discoid scrapers, blades, a

Fig. 28

broken polished axe) and a few sherds of a very coarse, unidentifiable pottery. The second megalithic tomb at Wéris is larger
than the first one, and has almost the same plan; but it is a
gallery-grave built on the ground and was originally covered
with an earth-mound. There, too, funerary chamber and ante-
chamber were separated by a stone slab pierced by a circular
opening. This tomb had already been robbed before excava-

Plate 32

tion, so that nothing is known about the grave-goods. One of
the two known but destroyed megaliths was a gallery-grave
at Jemeppe-Hargimont (Luxembourg), the other an indeter-
minate megalithic tomb at Velaine-lez-James (Namur).

Since the megalithic tombs seem to have been no more than
substitutes for natural caves, it is only natural that the SOM
people, when arriving in the Meuse valley and finding there a
population already practising collective burials in caves, should
adopt this same ritual so closely related to their own religious
ideas. In at least three caves, ossuaries have been found, the
grave-goods of which can undoubtedly be attributed to the
SOM civilization. The 'Trou des Blaireaux' at Vaucelles
(Namur) has yielded the bones of numerous individuals
together with many flint blades, polished flint axes—one of
these still with its stag-antler handle with transversal shaft-hole
—a transverse arrow-head, a lozenge-shaped arrow-head, a bone
point and sherds of three vessels, one of which could be put
together. It is a coarse, flat-bottomed bucket-pot with smooth
but undecorated surface, ovoid body and slightly widening

Fig. 27

neck. Also in this region, in the 'Trou des Blaireaux' at
Dourbes, a burial was found—unfortunately already robbed—
with some sherds of the same type of pottery. The cave at Ben-
Ahin contained the skeletons of fourteen individuals, arrow-
heads, flint scrapers and blades, two more Vaucelles-type pots
and a series of perforated teeth forming part of a necklace.
Lastly, during excavations a number of years ago, SOM pottery was discovered in two more caves of the Lesse valley: the

'Trou de la Naulette' at Walzin, and the 'Abri de la Poterie' at Hulsonniaux; it is, however, impossible to determine now whether these two caves had also been used as burial places. A number of other cave⁄ossuaries of the Meuse region, which have already been described, may also probably be attributed to the SOM civilization.

The only habitation site of the SOM civilization in the Low Countries was discovered at Rijckholt⁄Sint⁄Geertruid (Dutch

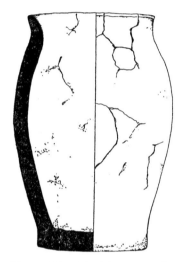

Fig. 27. Seine⁄Oise⁄Marne pottery from Vaucelles (prov. Namur). Height 8⅝ in.

Limburg, just across the Belgian frontier). It was an oval *fond⁄de⁄cabane* which yielded flint implements and some sherds of SOM pottery.

The two megalithic tombs at Wéris seem to have formed part of a big sacred ensemble. Indeed, over a distance of several kilometres and in a straight line orientated NNE–SSW are to be found successively a menhir, the larger gallery⁄grave, a second menhir, the smaller *allée couverte,* and lastly the three menhirs at Oppagne. While it is possible that these menhirs were set up during a later period—the Bronze Age—it is tempting to suppose that they were put there by the SOM people to form an imposing religious ensemble together with

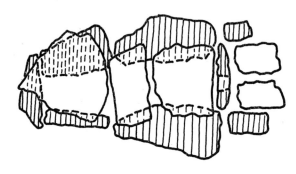

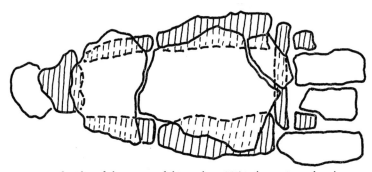

Fig. 28. Plan of the two megalithic tombs at Wéris (prov. Luxembourg). The larger 36 ft. long.

the megalithic tombs. More than ten menhirs can to this day be seen in Belgium, but their number must originally have been much larger. Their distribution area corresponds approxi-mately with the SOM area: Hainaut, the western part of the province of Namur and north of the province of Luxembourg. These monuments have never been systematically excavated,

but their religious character, although mysterious, is unques-
tionable. The region in which they are found in Belgium is
the most northerly part of the vast area of distribution of these
stone uprights, extending over the whole of north-western
France, from Brittany to the Oise, the Aisne and southern
Belgium. Amongst the most representative menhirs in our
country are the 'Pierre qui tourne' at Velaine-sur-Sambre, Plate 33
the 'Pierre qui tourne' at Baileux, the 'Zeupîre' at Gozée, the
'Pierre Brunehaut' between Hollain and Bléharies, the three
Oppagne menhirs at Wéris. The biggest of them all, the
'Longue Pierre' at Bray, was 22 ft. high, but unfortunately it
has been destroyed.

A last megalithic monument in Belgium must be mentioned, but this very probably dates from the Bronze Age. It is
the miniature 'Stonehenge' at Forrières (prov. Luxembourg).
This monument, known as 'Cuvelée du Diable', must have
been rather impressive. It comprised six small trilithons (each
formed by two orthostats and a horizontal lintel), standing in
a circle. About a century ago, only one of the eighteen stones
was missing, but the lintels had already fallen down. Today,
however, only very few stones (between 40 and 80 in. long, 23
and 55 in. wide and 16 and 28 in. thick) are left. Trial excavations, carried out at the beginning of this century, have shed
no light on the age of the monument.

In the Low Countries contacts had probably been established between the SOM people and the Beaker people.
Conceivably some Beaker elements went to the south: here
might be mentioned the discovery of a few battle-axes to the
south of the Beaker area, the presence of a pot-beaker in the
'Abri des Aulnes' at Dave (Namur), and lastly, the introduction into the SOM area of a grave-type borrowed from the
Beaker people, mainly in the Entre-Sambre-et-Meuse and on
the heights bordering the Famenne depression: inhumation
under a barrow. In this region the mounds do not consist of

sand, but are cairns made of loose stones picked up in the neighbourhood; they are called '*marchets*'. These cairns continued to be the usual method of burial up till Roman times in the area just mentioned. They can be individual tombs, but may just as well contain two or three skeletons. It has also been established that one or two secondary inhumations may sometimes be found inside an older *marchet*. We must mention the three cairns at Fagnolle (Namur), *marchet* No. II at Roly (Namur) and the *marchet* at Solre-sur-Sambre (Hainaut). The grave-goods were rather poor, namely a tanged arrow-head (Fagnolle I), an SOM-type beaker (primary grave at Fagnolle II), a tanged arrow-head, an amber bead and a few pottery sherds (secondary burial at Fagnolle II), a flint flake, three small flint blades and an SOM-type vessel (Fagnolle III), a long flint blade (Roly II). No grave-goods were discovered in the *marchets* Nos. I and III at Roly, but the skeletons seem to indicate that the typical neolithic rite of flesh-removal was practised.

Lastly, it may be mentioned that in several places of the SOM area in Belgium, Breton-type polished axes and axes in hard rock (jadeite, chloromelanite, nephrite) have been found, probably pointing to trade relations with the south and the south-west. Grand-Pressigny daggers, found as far north as Drenthe and as far east as the Aachen region, as well as amber beads found in the SOM and beaker regions, equally illustrate the active trade relations which, even at that period, connected Western and North-western Europe by the Atlantic route.

CHAPTER VII

The Bronze Age

THE TRANSITION BETWEEN the late Neolithic Period and the Bronze Age was, in the Low Countries, a very gradual one. Slowly the different cultures, described in the previous chapters, amalgamated to form a cultural whole in which the several constituent elements become very difficult to distinguish. The climate has changed, and the moderate continental conditions of the Subboreal have succeeded the Atlantic. Less rain, colder winters, warmer and drier summers are characteristic. The area covered with forest has diminished considerably, and where it subsists, beech gradually takes the place of lime. The marshes typical of the Atlantic have dried up, and their place is taken by large heaths; heather moors also appear in the spaces left open by the retreat of the forest, mainly in the sandy areas. Land communications and therefore trade become easier, thanks to this retreat of the forest and the drying up of the marshes. However, while many European countries —Ireland, southern England (Wessex culture), Brittany, Central Europe (Aunjetitz and Toszeg cultures), Denmark—lived in a period of remarkable wealth during the Bronze Age, this was not the case with the Low Countries. Here none of the raw materials on which these other countries based their wealth are to be found: copper, tin, gold, amber. For this reason, the new international traderoutes did not pass through our regions, inhabited as they were only by poor farmers having infrequent contacts with their neighbours, and visited occasionally by some travelling tradesmen selling bronze weapons and implements, jewellery and articles of dress. Such objects are scarce here, and the impression gained from a study of the Bronze Age in our regions is one of extreme poverty, in sharp contrast to the wealth of neighbouring countries. Only the last phase of

H

this period indicates a greater prosperity, and that is only relative.

Because of this poverty, a detailed chronological system—like the Montelius chronology of Northern Europe—is not possible for the Low Countries. We must be satisfied with a rather vague division into two phases, Early Bronze Age and Middle Bronze Age on one hand (1600 B.C.–1100 B.C., equivalent to Montelius I, II and III), and Late Bronze Age on the other (1100–650 B.C., equivalent to Montelius IV, V and VI). The Montelius chronology will be used only where more precise datings are possible.

It is certain that importing these first bronze implements had but little influence upon the way of life of the majority of the inhabitants, who continued to use flint, bone and antler as before. Only a few privileged persons were able to acquire metal objects; these were considered to be so valuable that flint imitations were immediately made. Polished axes have been found—for example at Maisières (Hainaut) and at Drachten (Frisia)—whose fan-shaped cutting edges clearly point to bronze prototypes. The same is true of a stone battle-axe found in Barrow I of Zuidwolde (Drenthe). Several nordic-type flint daggers, very finely made, found in the north of the Nether-lands, equally derive from metal weapons. This applies also to the flint sickle-blades of which relatively few have been discovered in the northern and western provinces of the Netherlands; they are crescent-shaped and their workmanship betokens an astonishing degree of skill. In 1934, quite a remarkable find was made at Heiloo (northern Holland): four flint sickle-blades were found together with a bronze one—probably an offering.

The first implements include flat bronze axes, still resembling the axes of polished stone. Only a dozen examples, found at

Fig. 29

widely separated places, are known from our regions (prov. Hainaut, Namur, East and West Flanders, Guelders, Overijssel). One of these was part of a founder's hoard discovered in 1841 at Wageningen (Guelders) and which also included two penannular bracelets and one spiral bracelet of bronze wire, a triangular daggerblade and the blade of an Irish halberd.

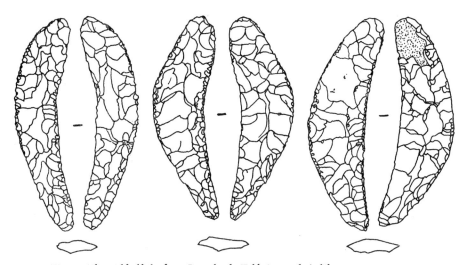

Fig. 29. Flint sickleblades from Grootebroek, Enkhuizen and Andijk (prov. North Holland), 1:3.

This hoard dates from Montelius I. The flanged axes, appearing a bit later, are more numerous, and they have been found all over the territory of the Low Countries, except in the Ardennes—where Bronze Age finds are extremely scarce. During the Middle Bronze Age, palstaves are relatively common, again except in the Ardennes. The founder's hoard at Voorhout (southern Holland) contained seventeen axes of this type, together with a flanged axe and a chisel. Most of the bronze axes of the first phases of the Bronze Age seem to have a Breton, English, Welsh or Irish origin. Not only bronze axes, but also stone ones were imported during this period, e.g. the battle-axe from Baexem (Dutch Limburg), coming perhaps from Central Europe, and the top of the partially preserved wooden shaft of which was decorated with small nails and little bronze plaques. Lastly, in Belgium, five or six axes made from hard rock (jadeite, chloromelanite, nephrite) have been found, imported from Brittany, where they are typical of the Armorican Early Bronze civilization. In our country, they date either from the end of the late Neolithic, or from the Early Bronze Age. The most beautiful example comes from Havenne (prov. Namur), and is $12\frac{1}{2}$ in. long.

As regards the metal weapons, it must be remembered that the Bell-beaker people had already introduced the copper dagger. Bronze daggers are extremely scarce in the Low Countries. However, the rather exceptional specimen from Bargeroostervelde (Drenthe), found in a peat-bog and dating from the Early Bronze Age, deserves special mention. The triangular blade is fastened by means of four bronze rivets to the horn-handle, the pommel of which is decorated with small tin nails. It seems to have been imported from the Aunjetizt area. One or two daggers from the same period were discovered in barrow-burials (e.g. at the Doornwertse Heide); one is part of the Wageningen hoard (cf. *supra*), another was found in the cave at Han.

Plate 36

During the Middle Bronze Age the sword appears, first rather short (for example, the sword from Zwijndrecht, East Flanders, perhaps imported from Lower Saxony), later longer. Some of them are imports from Ireland (for example, the ones found at Gottem, East Flanders; Wichelen, East Flanders; and Antwerp), others from Lower Saxony (like the two from the Overloon hoard, Dutch Limburg). This founder's hoard also included a bronze pin, a nicked flanged axe and two spear-heads which had probably been imported from Schleswig-Holstein.

Lastly, toilet-sets and jewellery have not only been found in graves, but also as stray finds. Only the most typical and the most exceptional will be mentioned here. A barrow at Weerdinge (Drenthe) contained two wheel-headed pins, a *Rollkopfnadel,* a disc-headed pin, a finger-ring, a penannular bracelet (all these objects in bronze) and a fine necklace of large amber beads (Montelius II). At Merendree (East Flanders) another disc-headed pin was found, 1 ft. long, and perhaps imported from Central Europe. Mention must be made of the famous necklace from Exloo-Odoorn (Drenthe), composed of 25 tin beads of English origin, 14 amber beads from the Baltic and 4 Egyptian segmented faience beads, giving a date of approximately 1400 B.C. Amongst the gold ornaments is a broken torque made of thin gold wire, with ends hammered flat, found in 1891 at Bennekom, and the small spiral rings found in the Galgenberg, a barrow between Sleen and Zweeloo (Drenthe), together with a palstave and fourteen bronze arrow-heads (Montelius II). In Belgium we have the Irish *lunula* from Fauvillers (Luxembourg), the Arlon torque (Luxembourg), rather similar to the above-mentioned Bennekom one, and two ear-rings from the burial-cave at Sinsin (Namur), prob-ably imported from England. Strangely enough, these three exceptional finds were made in the Ardennes, one of the regions where the Bronze Age civilization is at its poorest! Last of all must be mentioned the gold bracelet, weighing 252 gr., dredged from the River Scheldt at Wichelen (eastern Flanders).

This survey of the main imported objects during the Early and Middle Bronze Age indicates trade relations with Lower Saxony, Schleswig-Holstein and Denmark in the north, Central Europe in the east, Brittany in the south, and England, Wales and Ireland in the west. However, it is with England that these relations seem to have been most important. We will have to talk about them again later.

Fig. 30

Plate 24

Plate 34

Plate 35

Plate 38

Fig. 30. Disc-headed pin from Merendree (East Flanders). Length: 11¾ in.

Very few habitation sites of this period are known, and even less have been satisfactorily excavated. Some marsh villages in Flanders, such as Dentergem, already inhabited during the Neolithic, continue to be occupied in the Bronze Age. The same is true for the entrance of the Han caves in the Ardennes. Our information is limited to these few points. On the other hand, we know much more about graves and burial-rites, at least for some regions, like Drenthe, the Veluwe and North Brabant, where numerous and systematic excavations have been conducted; our information is more fragmentary for the other areas of the Netherlands and for Campine and Flanders in Belgium. It is almost entirely lacking for the other parts of Belgium; the most we can say is that to the south-east of the Meuse individual graves under cairns probably are still in use. Everywhere else individual barrow-graves, as known already from the late Neolithic Period, continue to be built. However, due to changes in the climate and flora, from now on these barrows are made of heather sods—this in the sandy areas— which distinguishes them very clearly from the sand-tumuli of the late Neolithic. As well as inhumation, which was the rule in late neolithic times, the rite of cremation appears. In some regions, as in Drenthe, the transition from inhumation to cremation is very gradual: originally the dead were buried in long oak cists, made by the hollowing out of a trunk by means of fire; later, cremation becomes more general and the burnt bones are deposited in a tree-coffin of the type already described. Slowly the dimensions of cist and grave decrease, and at last the bones are deposited in a shallow grave, together with pieces of charcoal from the pyre, while a mound is built over the grave. A last phase is the erection of a grave-mound over the pyre itself. More to the south, however, in northern Brabant, Campine and Flanders, cremation appears already in the Early Bronze Age, and is practised side by side with inhuma- tion, so that, although the same grave-types are to be found

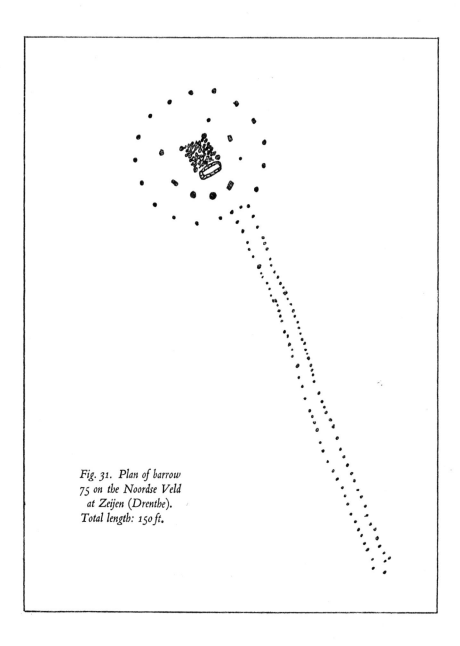

Fig. 31. Plan of barrow 75 on the Noordse Veld at Zeijen (Drenthe). Total length: 150 ft.

there as in Drenthe, neither evolution nor chronology are parallel. The structure of the graves is an evolution of the late neolithic barrows. In Drenthe, some barrows are still being built according to megalithic traditions: circular or oval, with sometimes the burial itself either in a rudimentary stone cist or in an oak coffin covered by a stone packing; others have a stone revetment. A typical example is the elongated barrow at Weerdinge (Drenthe), with a stone revetment and enclosing two burials with stone packing; this barrow calls to mind the megalithic tomb on the Schimmeres at Emmen already described. It must be noted, however, that similar structures are to be found also in other regions, outside the distribution area of the Funnel-beaker culture, such as the frontier region of Belgium, the Netherlands and Germany, in the south of Dutch Limburg and near Aachen, as well as in Flanders near the Mont de l'Enclus. Much more numerous are the barrows with peripheral wooden structures and (or) a ditch. These wooden structures are very varied and only the most typical can be mentioned here: widely spaced post-circles, peripheral palisades, widely spaced paired post-circles, simple closely spaced post-circles, double, triple (sometimes even quadruple or multiple)

Plate 38

closely spaced post-circles. They can also be combined with a peripheral ditch. It has been noted that often these post-circles had an opening (entrance?) which was later blocked, presumably

Fig. 31

for ritual purposes. In barrow 75 at the 'Noordse Veld' at Zeijen (Drenthe), traces have been discovered of two parallel rows of posts leading to the barrow and calling to mind the *alignements* of Brittany and the Stonehenge Avenue. Lastly, in a few barrows, the grave was protected by a temporary light wooden construction (a 'mortuary house') which was destroyed before the building of the mound. On the other sites, traces of funeral feasts and of 'ritual pits'—probably used for sacrifices—have been found. The already complicated structure of these barrows has been made even more difficult to interpret, because extant grave-mounds have frequently been re-used for later burials; on these occasions they were heightened and a new peripheral structure was added. In other cases, secondary graves have been dug into the sides of the barrow. Grave-goods are often lacking, or are very poor: small, crudely made vessels with uneven surface—sometimes decorated with nail impressions and rather like the SOM pottery—or a bronze weapon, implement or toilet-article. Only in a few tumuli were the grave-goods somewhat richer; for example, at Weerdinge, already mentioned, or at a barrow with stone revetment at Drouwen (Drenthe), with a 'mortuary house' (the oldest known up to now) and unusually rich grave-furniture: a bronze dagger of Sögel type, a tanged laurel leaf razor, a bronze flanged axe, two gold spirals, nine flint arrow-heads and a roughly worked flint artefact (Montelius I).

Notwithstanding this poverty, and thanks to the study of the barrow structure, it has been possible to reconstruct a number of ritual acts performed by the Bronze Age inhabitants of the Low Countries, and, in this way, to get an insight into their mentality and their beliefs. Only one example will be given, namely tumulus 8 of the Toterfout-Halve Mijl cemetery at Veldhoven (northern Brabant). The dead person was first cremated on a pyre and the burnt bones deposited in a shallow oval pit, together with pieces of charcoal from the pyre. This pit was covered by a temporary structure, the 'mortuary house', consisting of a light roof supported by four stakes. This mortuary house was then enclosed by a circle of slender stakes, probably carrying a fence of hurdles. The members of the family or clan then held a funeral feast near the grave and burnt a ritual fire. A few days later the mortuary house and the palisade were removed, and on top of the grave a heather-sod barrow was built, the base of which was surrounded with a peripheral circle consisting of sixteen widely-spaced posts, with an opening to the south. This 'entrance' was then blocked by more posts, and on this occasion a new ritual fire was burnt. After a lapse of some years, the tumulus was again used. A new cremation burial on its crest called for an enlargement of the barrow, its foot at the same time being surrounded by a double closely-spaced post-circle, left open over a distance of about two metres on the south-west side; this entrance was later blocked. Lastly, the whole of the mound was surrounded by an enclosing circle of close-set slender stakes, linked by horizontal hurdling. Almost every barrow has a different structure and reveals traces of varied ritual acts, related to the ones just described. Osteological examination of the cremated bones has brought to light a surprising fact: many of these monumental graves with complex structure have been built either for women, or for young children, or again for women who died in childbirth (bones of women found mixed with bones of newborn children or foetus). It has been suggested—and perhaps not without reason—that these elaborate tombs were built especially for people whose death presented some evil aspect, which made necessary this complicated magico-religious ritual, as an escape from the evil eye or to prevent the dead person from haunting the living. As regards the other dead, it is probable that they were buried in simple flat graves, without structure or grave-goods, which has often been the reason why they have not been recognized. In some cases, however, such Bronze Age graves have been discovered and dated. At the Mont de l'Enclus (Ruien, East Flanders), such an Early Bronze Age cremation burial without grave-goods had been cut into and partly destroyed during the erection of a cremation barrow with peripheral ditch, which was heightened later for a new burial and enclosed by a stone revetment. Later again, a secondary grave was dug into the body of the mound, consisting of a cremation burial inside a Hilversum urn (see under), dating from the Middle Bronze Age (end of Montelius II or Montelius III) and of which more will be said presently.

Fig. 32

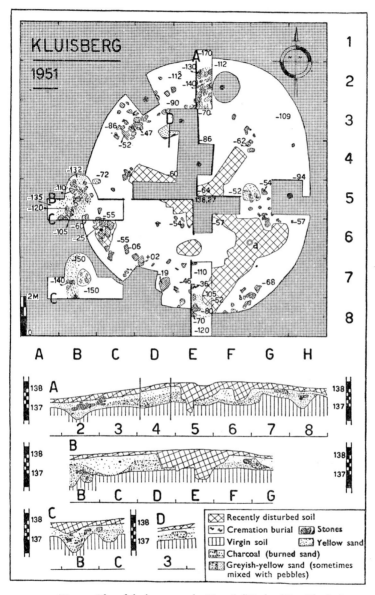

Fig. 32. Plan of the barrow on the Mont de l'Enclus (East Flanders).

Up to now, we have only considered the culture, during the Early and Middle Bronze Age, of the inhabitants of the Low Countries descended from the late neolithic population. At the end of the Montelius II period, however, a new element reinforced the autochthonous population. Since late neolithic times and the migration of part of the Bell-beaker people to England, intensive relations existed between that country and our own regions. These contacts can be seen, for instance, in a certain similarity between the construction of some Dutch barrows and English ones, and also in important trading. Between 1400 and 1200 B.C., population elements from England crossed the Channel, and, coming by a route marked by pottery finds from the region of Boulogne and the hills of southern Flanders (Mont de l'Enclus), established themselves in Campine and North Brabant, while two other groups went to the Nymegen and Hilversum regions respectively. Sporadic traces of these newcomers were also found in the west of the Netherlands, near The Hague. They brought with them a new burial ritual: the dead were cremated and the bones deposited in an urn which was placed, sometimes inverted, in the grave. These rather coarsely made 'Hilversum' urns are generally of rather large dimensions; the body is either ovoid or bucket-shaped, sometimes slightly carinated; the base is thick and the foot well defined. In most cases, a relief band with fingertip- or nail-impressions, sometimes between two shallow parallel grooves, is to be seen an inch or two under the rim. The zone between relief band and rim is decorated with cord-impressions sometimes forming a basketry pattern, sometimes a chevron or trellis pattern. Another urn, sherds of which were discovered at Budel (North Brabant) merits special attention, because its shoulder was decorated with five horse-shoe handles in relief, characteristic of certain English urns. About the same time appears in the Low Countries a new type of barrow, equally of English origin: the tumulus with circular ditch and

Plate 37

Fig. 33

external or internal bank. They are mainly to be found in North Brabant and Belgian Campine, but an isolated example exists in the north of the Netherlands (in Drenthe), and to the south others are known from Belgian Brabant and from the north of Hainaut. Although the area of distribution of these barrows does not coincide exactly with that of the Hilversum urns, it seems probable that they were introduced by the same immigrants. Indeed, the primary grave of the twin-barrow 1^B of

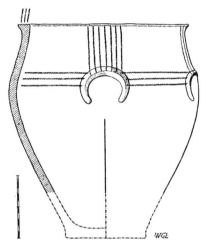

Fig. 33. Urn with horse-shoe handles from Budel (North Brabant). Height: 14 in.

the Toterfout-Halve Mijl necropolis, with bank and ditch, contained a cremation burial in an urn of this type. This bar-row has been dated by pollen analysis and C-14 and confirms the arrival of the newcomers at some time between 1400 and 1200 B.C. Peaceful contacts were immediately established with the native population, because numerous descendants of the Hilversum urns have been discovered in secondary graves dug into already existing barrows, while on the other hand some of the older inhabitants adopted the new type of grave; for example at Postel (Belgian Limburg), the primary grave of a ditch-and-bank barrow consisted of a cremation in an oak-cist. It has been possible to establish a relative chronology thanks to the evolution of some elements of the Hilversum urns (for instance, the shape of the rim). During the Late Bronze Age, the cord-impressed decoration disappears, this new type being known as a Drakenstein urn. Their area of distribution is larger than that of the Hilversum urns, and extends from Flanders in the south (Mont de l'Enclus region and Scheldt valley) to Drenthe in the north. The three main zones, however, remain the same as for the Hilversum urns: Campine and North Brabant, Nymegen region and Hilversum region. The Drakenstein urns are mostly found in secondary burials dug into Early and Middle Bronze Age barrows, but in the Urnfields they are no longer to be seen. Therefore they must be dated from the first phase of the Late Bronze Age (Montelius IV). Some native elements have also adopted the cremation burials in urns; indeed, during this period—even before the arrival of the Urnfield folk—one finds, in Drenthe and the Veluwe, cremations in very crudely shaped pots, without decoration or relief ornaments, which seem to be local imitations of the Hilversum-Drakenstein urns.

At the 'Wezelsche Bergen' at Wijchen (Guelders), sherds of Hilversum urns were found in connection with traces of square houses, while very recently a Late Bronze Age habitation site, with pottery which has a great deal in common with the Drakenstein-urn family, has been excavated at the Margijnen Enk, near Deventer (Overijssel). Traces of a rectangular house, 50 by 16 ft., with two hearths, have been discovered there. It is to be noted that the vessels for these people's everyday use are the same as the funerary pottery. It has been observed that the rims of many Hilversum-Drakenstein urns show blackish traces of organic material—cooked food—which shows that the pots were first used as kitchen ware before being utilized as funerary urns![1]

Plates 39, 40

The Drakenstein urns have brought us to the Late Bronze Age. A clear distinction is apparent between the beginning of this period (Montelius IV)—which in many ways is only a continuation of the Middle Bronze Age—and its final phase (Montelius V and VI).[2] This last is characterized by new invasions and by important cultural changes. At the end of this chapter we will examine the arrival of these Urnfield populations.

Graves and burial ritual of the Montelius IV period have for a great part already been described: on one hand, the descendants of the English immigrants buried the cremated bones of their dead in Drakenstein urns, mostly as secondary burials in older barrows; under their influence part of the native population equally adopted the rite of urn-cremation. Other native groups, on the other hand, remained faithful to their old traditions: in Drenthe, it is the period of barrows erected over funeral pyres, elsewhere of ditch-barrows and (or) peripheral post- or stake-circles. Even during the final phase of the Bronze Age, when the Urnfield invasions will have appreciably changed the funeral ritual, traces of archaic rites and customs will still be found: at Sinsin (prov. Namur), for instance, collective burial in caves still exists, while at Ghent (Port-Arthur) an inhumation burial with rich grave-goods—to be discussed later—seems to date from the beginning of the Iron Age (Hallstatt C).

There is in the Low Countries considerable difference between the Late Bronze Age and the earlier phases: from the economic point of view, the material poverty of the preceding period gives way to a relative prosperity, which, however, cannot be compared with the astonishing wealth that characterizes other countries, like Brittany, northern Switzerland or Denmark. Bronze objects from this period are more numerous and their diverse origins (Brittany, north-west France, Great Britain, Denmark, Lower Saxony, Hanover, western Germany, northern Switzerland) point to trade relations with all these regions. It will be noted that the Scheldt area (Lowland Belgium and the south-western Netherlands) was mainly in contact with north-western France and Great Britain, while the area adjoining the River Meuse (middle and highland Belgium and the south-eastern Netherlands) imported objects from northern Switzerland, eastern France and western Germany. The northern provinces of the Netherlands depended mostly upon north-western Germany and even Denmark. These trade relations, however, were not at all exclusive, as will be shown later in the description of the most important finds. They continued during the whole of the final Bronze Age, and even during the beginning of the Iron Age. They were not hindered by the Urnfield invasions; it is quite possible that in some cases these invasions were even helpful.

The itinerant bronze smiths travelled more often through our regions[3] and the founder's hoards are more numerous and much richer. They have been discovered all over the Low Countries, and only the most important will be mentioned here. One of the most remarkable is the hoard from Drouwen (Drenthe), composed mainly of ornamental objects (bronze, glass-paste and jet necklace beads, buckles, bracelets, rings, etc.), partly northern imports (a damaged *Haengekar*—the only one found up to now in the Low Countries—a spectacle fibula, spiral rings), partly western imports (for example, seven massive omega-shaped bracelets). Another rich hoard is that of Bergen-Terblijt (Dutch Limburg), with a palstave, two winged axes, a few socketed axes, two spear-heads, several sickle blades, bracelets, etc. Twenty socketed axes were found at Hoogstraten (prov. Antwerp) and twenty-six at Geistingen (Ophoven, Belgian Limburg). The find at Jemeppe-sur-Sambre (Hainaut) was composed of four socketed axes, two penannular 'palette'-bracelets, several small bronze rings and bronze and tin spiral tubes. Lastly, at Dave (prov. Namur), a small hoard contained four big twisted torques of a type found in southern England and West Europe, from the Channel to the north-west of the Continent. Occasionally bronze objects were made in our own regions, as is shown by a casting-mould for socketed axes, found in Drenthe.

Amongst the most typical objects are the winged axe and the socketed axe. The first is related to the civilizations of Central Europe and has been found mainly in the Meuse valley, but also in the Scheldt area and even Picardy. It does not occur in the northern provinces of the Netherlands. As regards the socketed axes, some, with quadrangular section, seem to have their origin in Brittany; only a few of these have been found in Belgium. Most of the socketed axes are of a type whose distri- bution area covers, apart from the Low Countries, Lower Saxony and south-eastern England: some are decorated with imitation wings calling to mind the winged axes, others with parallel ridges. The other bronze implements include a few sickle blades (some of which come from northern Switzer- land) and socketed chisels. A few tanged knives with geo- metric ornamentation, again from northern Switzerland, have been found, for instance in the cave at Sinsin and at Mohin- ville (prov. Namur). From the northern part of the Nether- lands (Valthe, Vroomshoop and Appelsga, Frisia—which yielded a particularly fine piece) come knives with handle and blade cast in one piece, both geometrically decorated. The dis- tribution area of the knives of this type is limited to the north of the Netherlands and north-western Germany (Ems-Weser). The same opposition can be seen as regards the razors: the Nordic type has been found in the Netherlands (for example, in the secondary burials in a barrow at Harenermolen (Gronin- gen) and as far as Sittard (Dutch Limburg); this last one is decorated with a stylized ship. From the Meuse valley and in Belgian Brabant, on the contrary, a few double-edged razors with annular handle, of Swiss origin (Sinsin cave, urnfields at

Plate 44

Biez and Court-Saint-Etienne) are known. A razor of this type has even been discovered as far north as the urnfield at Gasteren (Drenthe). As regards the weapons, the rather numerous swords must be mentioned, found mainly in two regions: the Scheldt valley (East Flanders), on the one hand, Dutch Limburg and the adjacent part of Guelders and of the Meuse valley, on the other. Most of these are tanged swords (*Griffzungenschwerter*) of different types. A few seem to have come from north-western France (the carp's tongue swords from Hamme (East Flanders) and Nijmegen (Guelders), and the one of an earlier type found at Melle (East Flanders)); others, such as those from Gentbrugge (East Flanders) and Nijmegen (Guelders) are of English origin. Most of these swords, however, seem to have been imported from western Central Europe (Middle Rhine, south-western Germany, northern Switzerland) and date from the Montelius IV and V periods: swords from Ertvelde, Dikkelvenne, Melle, Oude-naarde, etc. (East Flanders), swords from Tegelen, Venlo, Maastricht, Bossefeld, Steenwijk, etc. (Dutch Limburg, Overijssel and Guelders). Only very few examples come from other areas. Finally, mention must be made of the massive-handled swords (*Vollgriffschwerter*) from North Brabant, one of the Auvergnier type and two of the Möringen type. Spear-heads are not scarce either, and have been found almost every-where. A few large specimens from the Scheldt valley (Oude-naarde, Geraardsbergen, Ghent, Duffel) and from Groningen and Drenthe are English imports or have been made in north-western France after English prototypes.

Lastly, of the ornaments—apart from the objects from the already described founder's hoards—mention must be made of bracelets, pins of different types, and penannular palette-bracelets. While the Han cave habitation (prov. Namur) has yielded a palette-bracelet of Swiss import, other similar pieces with big palettes, probably made in the Picardy-Scheldt region after Swiss prototypes, have been found in the Scheldt area (Spiennes, Jemeppe-sur-Sambre, Ghent, Zandbergen, Schoonaarde) and in north-western France (Picardy). This brings us to the grave discovered at Port-Arthur (Ghent) which, although dating from the beginning of the Iron Age (Hallstatt C), can still be placed in the general context of the final Bronze Age trade relations. This female inhumation-grave, of which unfortunately the structure has not been observed, contained relatively rich grave-goods, all bronze objects: two bracelets with big palettes, a big spiral which is probably the head of a very large spiral-pin, a spiral brooch, two hangers, an ear-ring, two necklace beads, a hemispherical button, a perforated disc and thirty-six rings. Most of these objects come from the Atlantic coastal area, but the spiral-headed pin and the double spiral-brooch seem to indicate trade with more distant regions (Prussia and Poland).

Plate 46

It has been suggested that the finds of the Scheldt region are the remains of a well-defined civilization, characterized both by its military aspect (numerous weapons) and the existence of typical ornaments (bracelets with big palettes). However, these last can be explained by the activity of local craftsmen, imitating Swiss prototypes, while the abundance of weapons is equally true for the south-eastern Netherlands (Dutch Limburg and South Guelders) and may perhaps have its origin in the presence in these regions of a warrior and merchant aristocracy, whose armament is in clear contrast with the peaceful character of the farmers and herdsmen who formed the most important elements of the population at that time. Also, the most typical remains of the Bronze Age civilizations already described are found as well in the Scheldt area as in the region of Nijmegen: palisade-barrow civilization, Hilversum-Drakenstein civilization, and lastly, during the final Bronze Age, the Urnfield civilization.

At the end of the Bronze Age, the cultural aspect of nearly the whole of Europe was revolutionized by vast movements of people, of which even a summary description cannot be attempted here. Suffice it to say that the origin of these migrations must be sought in the Lausitz area, and started at about 1100 B.C. Our regions, however, were affected around the eighth century B.C. Amongst these immigrants, a clear distinction must be made between those who occupied the area situated to the north of the big Rhine bend (Overijssel, Drenthe, Groningen, Frisia) and those more to the south. Indeed, the Lausitz migrations started on their way quite a number of very different peoples, having in common only the burial ritual, borrowed from the Lausitz civilization: the dead were cremated, the ashes deposited in an urn and buried either in a flat grave, or under a low barrow; these graves were grouped in vast cemeteries. For this reason, all these peoples are known as Urnfield peoples. Notwithstanding this common funeral ritual, all the different populations kept certain individual characteristics, which are mainly apparent in their pottery. The immigrants occupying Hesbaye, Belgian Brabant, Flanders, Campine, Dutch Limburg and North Brabant came from southern Germany and northern Switzerland, having followed the Rhine. Together with their kinsmen established to the east of the Rhine, on the north and the south of the River Lippe, they formed what has become known as the 'Lower Rhine Urnfield group'. Certain pottery types (*infra*) call to mind, in a rather attenuated form, the Lausitz urns. On the other hand, the immigrants in the provinces to the north of the Rhine have their origin in Westphalia and Hanover, and their civilization, apart from the burial ritual, shows no element directly related to the Urnfield civilization *stricto sensu*. Both in the north and the south, the newcomers absorbed the native population, whose influence can, however, still be seen, for instance, in some elements of the grave-structure and in certain

ceramic forms. Furthermore, although of different origin, contacts had been established between the northern and the
southern group; we will have to talk about these later.

Most of the urnfields remained in use for several centuries.
Only the oldest graves—the Late Bronze Age ones—will be
described here; the Iron Age cemeteries belong to the next
chapter.

In the southern group, the tomb structure is not uniform,
but changes according to the regions. They are flat graves,
without internal structure, in Belgian Brabant (Novillesur
Méhaigne, Biez, CourtSaintEtienne) and in Flanders (Temse,
Aalter). At Biez, it is true, in some graves the urn was surrounded by a few big stones, while at CourtSaintEtienne
sometimes a schistplaque covered the mouth of the urn. More
to the north, in Campine, the burials were covered with rather
large but low mounds, without peripheral ditch; at least, this
was the case at LommelKattenbos, the other cemeteries
(Neerpelt, Overpelt, Grobbendonk, etc.) not having been dug
in a scientific manner. Lastly, in the southern Netherlands
(Limburg and North Brabant), the graves were also covered
with a low barrow, but with a shallow peripheral ditch around
the base (Riethoven, Bergeik, Luiksgestel, Best, Goirle,
Vlodrop, etc.). The origin of this last structural element must
probably be sought in the Bronze Age barrowcivilization and
perhaps even in the Beaker cultures: it seems that this shallow
peripheral ditch has the same magical purpose as the ditches,
postcircles and palisades of the earlier period. The gravegoods
are very poor and consist generally only of the urn. Sometimes
this contains one or two small accessory vessels and very rarely
a bronze object, ornament or toilet article. For this reason the
tomb at Biez, containing a bronze pin, a razor and a pair of
tweezers, is exceptional, just as are the Grobbendonk grave
with a vaseheaded pin, and two graves in North Brabant, at
Best and Luiksgestel, both containing a necklace made of a

Plate 41

Plate 5

series of small bronze hangers of hollow conical shape. A tomb at Goirle must be mentioned, comprising five big urns buried upside down, one of which contained four pottery bowls, another a series of smaller vessels, and the three last ones the cremated bones; similar burials are also fairly frequently found in the Upper Rhine area, but are exceptional in our regions. The absence of weapons in these graves should be noted, which might indicate the peaceful character of the newcomers.

The pottery includes thin-walled urns with rounded base and cylindrical or slightly widening neck; sometimes they are decorated with an incised geometrical pattern on the shoulder and with shallow grooves on the body or horizontal lines separating neck and shoulder. Some examples have two small

Plate 42

handles at the base of the neck.

Going up the Rhine, these newcomers established contacts with the Middle Bronze Age population of Alsace and the Palatinate, characterized by a pottery with deeply incised ornamentation, forming zig-zag friezes and festoons. Part of this population accompanied the immigrants to the Low Countries and their *Kerbschnitt*-pottery has been found in several urnfields in the Low Countries: in Campine (Neerpelt), Dutch Limburg (Vlodrop, Baarlo) and in North Brabant (Bergeik,

Plate 43

Luiksgestel). One group went further north still, and debased vessels of that type were discovered in some urnfields of the northern provinces of the Netherlands (cf. *infra*).

Only one habitation site of the southern Urnfield people is known. At Lens-Saint-Servais (Hesbaye, prov. Liège), about seven habitations have been excavated; unfortunately the work was not done very well, and the plan of the 'houses' (*fonds de cabanes?*) is unknown. Apart from a clay spinning-whorl and a bronze pin, two types of vessels were found, one very coarse with occasional nail-impressed ornaments and rather like the SOM pottery, the other, on the contrary, very well made: bowls with roughened exterior but carefully smoothed interior;

sometimes with incised geometric decoration, and vases with grooves and slightly widening neck. This type of pot calls to mind the vessels of the Upper-Rhine and western Swiss urn-fields.

In the northern group, the oldest graves from the cemeteries in Overijssel, Drenthe, Groningen and Frisia (Oldenzaal, Gasteren, Vledder, Laudermarke, etc.) show an internal struc-ture going back almost certainly to the native Bronze Age civilization. They are rather low rectangular barrows sur-rounded by a rectangular ditch with rounded corners, the interior of which shows rectangular post-settings (perhaps of mortuary houses, or a low fence?). The grave itself contains either an inhumation or a cremation, with or without urn. Somewhat more recent are the urn-graves surrounded by a keyhole-shaped peripheral ditch, with sometimes an internal palisade in the penannular part. Contrary to the first graves, these last, rather scarce in the Netherlands (Sleen, Noordbarge, Emmen and Erica in Drenthe; Wessinghuizen, Jipsinghuizen and Wedderveer in Groningen), have their origin in West-phalia, where this type is more often found.

As in the southern group, the grave-goods of these tombs are extremely poor. The urns are either biconical or pear-shaped, with or without cylindrical or truncated cone-shaped neck, and sometimes with two small handles. They indicate clearly the Westphalo-Hanoverian origin of these new elements in the population. However, a few *Kerbschnitt*-urns of southern type also occur as isolated elements in Overijssel and Drenthe (cf. *supra*). In the next chapter more will be said about the later evolution of these cemeteries during the Iron Age.

Up to now no traces of Late Bronze Age urnfields have been found in two regions: the western provinces of the Nether-lands, and highland Belgium (Famenne and the Ardennes). This may appear strange for this last area, because beyond the south-east Belgian frontier, in the Trier region, another Urnfield

Plate 48

group is known, showing influences both of the south German and west Swiss group (*Rheinisch-Schweizerische Urnenfelderkultur*) and the group of Swabia and the Lower Main (*Untermainisch-Schwäbische Urnenfelderkultur*). The only sign of the Urnfield civilization in the Ardennes is a *Kerbschnitt*-bowl discovered in the Han cave habitation (Namur).

The present writer thinks that all too often an attempt has been made to give an ethnic explanation of some archaeological facts, usually without any secure basis whatsoever. Notwithstanding our reticence on this particular aspect, we must admit how very tempting it is to see in the southern Urnfield group of the Low Countries the Celts, and in the representatives of the northern group the Germans—the two important populations whose common frontier coincided approximately with the Lower Rhine at the time of the Roman conquest.

The Hallstatt Civilization

THE MIGRATIONS OF the Urnfield people still belong, in the Low Countries, to the final phase of the Bronze Age. During the same period, however, the use of iron, already known for a long time in the Near East and which from there had spread to Greece and Italy, made its appearance in Central Europe. In the Salzkammergut in Austria lived a people that specialized in salt-mining; intensive trade relations existed with Italy and more especially with the people of the Villanovan civilization. Over the Brenner pass numerous Mediterranean products—mainly bronze objects—were in this way imported into highland Austria, and due to the influence of these trade and cultural contacts—which became even more important during the following centuries—a flourishing civilization developed in the Salzburg area, the so-called Hallstatt culture. It is in this civilization that, during the eighth century B.C., iron gradually takes the place of bronze for the manufacture of weapons and tools. Through its considerable cultural importance and following several migrations, this Hallstatt civilization has strongly marked the Central and West European cultures during the first Iron Age. Amongst these, two merit special attention: one, the so-called Koberstadt culture, in Baden, on the Middle Rhine, the other in north-eastern France, the Jura, Franche-Comté and Côte d'Or. Both have a definite military character and indicate the presence in these regions of a warrior aristocracy, very probably Celtic, which by armed force had established a hold over the older native population, especially over the Urnfield people. The Hallstatt civilization of north-eastern France is characterized mainly by big grave mounds, where the dead were buried with their weapons, sometimes with their battle-chariot, toilet articles and precious objects imported from Italy (often Etruscan) and even from Greece: cauldrons, situlae, tripods and gold jewellery frequently occur.

About the middle of the seventh century B.C., a group of these warriors, having probably passed through Lorraine, but perhaps coming from Central Europe (certain of their type fossils, e.g. horse-trappings, may, indeed, indicate relationship with Bavaria) invaded part of central and highland Belgium (prov. Namur, Hainaut, Brabant), and established themselves there as rulers. This invasion marks, for our regions, the beginning of the Iron Age.

The only remains of this people found up to now are a series of cemeteries, but the grave-goods are rich and very typical. The most important are the cemeteries at Gedinne ('Chevaudos') and Louette-Saint-Pierre in the province of Namur, Havré and Harchies in Hainaut, Court-Saint-Etienne, Limal and Wavre in Brabant. A few badly excavated tombs from the hills in southern Flanders may be added. The cemeteries generally consist of quite a large number of rather big tumuli, which, in Brabant, are in marked contrast with the flat graves of the Urnfield people living in the same region about a century earlier. While their cousins from the Koberstadt culture and north-eastern France buried their dead in inhumation graves, the Hallstatt warriors from Belgium borrowed the cremation ritual from the native population. The pyre used for burning the dead man and part of his equipment was sometimes situated near the barrow, but very often this last was built over the pyre itself. These barrows, built of sods or sand, depending on the region, are without internal structure. Only one of the tumuli at Louette-Saint-Pierre had its base surrounded with big stones. The burnt bones were deposited in an urn, mostly pear-shaped and with a widening neck, clearly related to the Koberstadt pottery. In one of the Gedinne tombs, the ashes were not put into an urn, but enveloped with a thin sheet of bronze. Urn and grave-goods were placed on top of the charcoal of the pyre, the whole being covered by the burial mound. The grave-goods vary considerably from one tomb to the next; the richest are almost exclusively from men's graves. Inside the urn, or next to it, was sometimes placed a small accessory vessel; equipment is often found in the grave, deformed by the action of the fire: belt-buckles, fragments of shoulder-belts, pectoral discs, etc. Frequently the weapons of the dead man are buried, in most cases the sword. Some of these warriors still used the bronze sword (tanged sword of a late type), but others had the big and heavy Hallstatt C iron sword, the length of the blade alone sometimes exceeding 3¼ ft.; during the Hallstatt D period the shorter antenna sword appears. Only rarely was the sword intact when deposited in the grave: very frequently the bronze sword was broken, or the iron one ritually bent. Of the sheath only the chape is preserved. A Gedinne tomb contained a bronze spear-head. Some graves comprise a bronze razor with single or double rounded cutting edge, of a type found in north-eastern France; they are sometimes accompanied by a pair of small iron tweezers. It has been observed that in the Belgian Hallstatt tombs, razors and swords tend to be mutually exclusive; the reason for this remains unexplained. If the Hallstatt chariot-burials are, up to now, lacking in Belgium, some tombs at least contain a few horse trappings, like iron bits, bronze plaques and little bells. Lastly, bronze vessels are very scarce. One of the richest graves is doubtless the tumulus V at Court-Saint-Etienne, dating from Hallstatt D: it contained, apart from the cinerary urn and a few accessory vessels, an iron spear-head, a bronze socketed axe, a simple-edged, rather short sabre blade, an antenna sword, two iron horse-bits and an iron trident with curved tips, probably the *stimulus* of a charioteer.

A tomb with grave-goods rather resembling the Hallstatt objects from central Belgium and dating from Hallstatt D, was discovered at Oss in the Netherlands (North Brabant), quite a distance to the north of the occupation zone of the Hallstatt warriors just mentioned. It consists of a large tumulus with a diameter of about 170 ft. The cremated bones were deposited in a large bronze situla imported from Italy. A few bronze ornaments and rings were found, together with a whetstone, fragments of cloth and three weapons: the blade of a short sword (originally an antenna sword?), the blade of a single-edged sabre and a long iron sword, ritually bent and with the handle richly decorated with gold-sheet geometric motifs, fixed by means of small bronze rivets. Do we have here the grave of a warrior coming from the south and killed during a raiding expedition, or does it belong to a native chieftain converted to the Hallstatt way of life? We are rather inclined to adopt the second possibility. Indeed, the structure of the tomb—if the interpretation given by the excavators is correct—presents certain aspects characteristic of the native burials (cf. *infra*): traces were found of two concentric ditches, one of which surrounds the grave itself, the other encircling the base of the barrow. The grave-goods were probably commercial imports. The same is true of several bronze tanged swords of a late type, found in the south of the Netherlands, e.g. Heusden (North Brabant), Montfort (Limburg), Rhenen (Guelders), of the bronze antenna sword from Onnen (Groningen), and of the bronze situlae from Baarlo (Dutch Limburg) and Ede (Guelders), coming from Italy. The bronze bucket from Meppen (Drenthe) on the other hand seems to be of Nordic origin.

This leads us to consider the situation during the same period in northern Belgium and the Netherlands. The archaeological remains indicate an essentially peaceful culture, in marked contrast with the warrior-civilization of central Belgium. The clear distinction between the areas north and south of the Rhine

that existed during the final phase of the Bronze Age, has remained and appears even more accentuated.

In the region occupied by the southern group (Dutch and
Belgian Limburg, North Brabant, prov. Antwerp, Flanders),
several final Bronze Age urnfields continue to be used, while
at the same time numerous new ones are established. They are
mainly to be found in Belgian Campine and North Brabant
and indicate an increase of the population, probably due to new
immigrations. These may have been initiated by the advance
to the south and west of the Germanic peoples of the northern
group, about whom more will be said later.

As during the previous period, the tomb-structure varies
with the region. In North Brabant (e.g. at Uden) and in Dutch
Limburg (e.g. the cemetery of the Hamert, near Venlo), the
tombs are surrounded by a peripheral ditch with magico-
religious significance. During the Hallstatt D period, this
circular ditch sometimes has a break in it, which was probably
the symbolic entrance to the tomb. In one case (at Uden), four
post-holes forming a rectangle were seen inside this 'entrance',
suggesting the existence of a small shrine.

More to the south, in the Belgian Campine (e.g. at Lommel-
Kattenbos), the barrows without peripheral ditch of the previous period still exist, but gradually become smaller. The same
characteristics are to be seen in several cemeteries of the Rhine
area, as at Rheinberg and Issum. Secondary graves are frequently found near the base or in the side of the barrows of these
first two groups.

Lastly, in the northern part of Belgian Brabant (e.g. at
Aarschot-Langdorp) and in Flanders (e.g. at Temse and
Aalter), the cemeteries are characterized by flat, structureless
graves.

The grave-goods are extremely poor. Apart from the funerary
urn, sometimes with a dish placed upside down as lid, occasionally one or two small accessory vessels are placed inside the

urn with the burnt bones, and exceptionally an ornament or toilet article is found (spiral ring, bronze bracelet, etc.) Tomb 20 of Lommel-Kattenbos, with its urn, whetstone, iron razor, iron tweezers and a small forked toilet article (*Hautkratzer*), represents one of the richer finds!

Gradually the funerary rites change. While at the beginning the burnt bones are carefully collected and deposited in the urn, charcoal from the pyre and bones are now found mixed together inside it, while other fragments of bone and charcoal are scattered around the funerary vessel (*Brandschüttungsgrab*). This evolution continued into the La Tène period, with tombs where traces of the pyre itself are mixed with the grave-goods (*Brandgrubengrab*) and others where the burnt bones are buried without an urn but simply wrapped in a piece of cloth (*Knochenlager*).

Plate 42

Several types of pottery are found. The most characteristic urns, however, resemble those from the already described Hallstatt warrior-graves: they have a pear-shaped body and widening neck and are derived from the Koberstadt culture, by way of the Laufeld culture from the Eifel region. Hallstatt D also sporadically yielded a few urns with oblique and horizontal grooving, the so-called 'Kalenderberg' decoration. Near Oss (North Brabant), at Posterholt (Dutch Limburg) and at Wijchen (Guelders), several graphite-painted urns with geometric ornamentation (festoons and chevrons) have been found, which seem to date from the Hallstatt D period; they are related to the same sort of pottery from the Rhineland. A separate place is reserved for the notched-rimmed and truncated pear-shaped vessels of Harpstedt type. They date from Hallstatt C/D and were discovered both in secondary graves dug into Bronze Age barrows and in urnfields. In these last, however, when the cemeteries consist of graves with a peripheral ditch and where careful observation has been possible, it appeared that they were not enclosed by peripheral ditches. It has been suggested that they are specifically Germanic, but we prefer another explanation, later put forward by Bursch and adopted by Glasbergen, namely that they are derived from the Middle and Late Bronze Age Hilversum-Drakenstein urns and must therefore be attributed to the descendants of the older native populations. These urns are relatively numerous in the southern group area, mainly in Dutch Limburg, North Brabant and Campine (e.g. the Hamert, Overpelt, Neerpelt, Grobbendonk, etc.), but they also occur in the northern group.

Mention must now be made of the southern cemetery of Lommel-Kattenbos, dating from the final Bronze Age and the Hallstatt C/D period, and consisting of barrows without peripheral ditch. At both the eastern and the western limits of this cemetery, traces were found of two remarkable monuments: post-holes suggesting a small rectangular construction, surrounded by a ditch, but without burial. They very probably are little sanctuaries with a funerary significance. Similar observations have been made in several cemeteries of the northern group, but these seem to be later and date from La Tène times (cf. *infra*).

Little is known of the habitations in the southern zone during the Hallstatt period. The best known site is at Rekem (Belgian Limburg), where traces were discovered of several huts, whose plan unfortunately could not be reconstructed. Pavements of irregular big stones, with their interstices filled with small pebbles, were found, together with hearths situated next to these floors, traces of wattle-and-daub, a grinding stone, loom-weights and pottery identical to the vessels found in the graves, among them a vase with Kalenderberg decoration. At Lommel (Hoever Heide) (Belgian Limburg) we have excavated the remains of two hut sites. Unfortunately, the area had been disturbed rather badly during recent years, but certain indications suggest a rectangular plan. The pottery is very much like the ware from the Lommel-Kattenbos necropolis, lying close by, which makes possible a date of final Hallstatt–early La Tène. At Arnhem, a habitation site has been excavated yielding sherds of a vase with Kalenderberg decoration: a rectangular house was found, 33 by 16 ft., with central hearth and subdivided into several rectangular rooms.

Lastly, traces of Iron Age fields were discovered in North Brabant. They are similar to the ones found in the northern zone; more will be said about them later.

Now the area situated north of the Rhine. There, too, the cemeteries have become more numerous and they have extended to the west and the south. The Lippe valley, which during the final Bronze Age formed part of the southern group, is now occupied by peoples belonging to the northern group. This fact is probably related to the expansion of the Germanic peoples who will reach the Lower Rhine during the La Tène period.

Plate 47

In the cemeteries, the largest number of graves now have a round peripheral ditch (sometimes even a double one), in some cases accompanied with a palisade, either external (as at Oldenzaal in Overijssel) or internal (as at Laudermarke, prov. Groningen). These wooden structures disappear gradually. The pottery has the same typical shapes as during the preceding period (biconical or pearshaped urns with or without cylindrical or conical neck), but slowly they become less accentuated. Harpstedt urns also occur (for example, at Vledder, in Drenthe); these, as has already been shown, derive from the Bronze Age HilversumDrakenstein urns. Urns with Kalenderberg decoration are more scarce (Vledder provides an example). The gravegoods have become even poorer than during the final Bronze Age.

Like their southern kinsmen, these people were for the most part agriculturalists. Grainimpressions in pottery show that they knew wheat, oats, barley, millet; rye, on the other hand, does not seem to have been cultivated at that time. Numerous

traces of Iron Age fields have been discovered—mainly thanks
to air photography—in Drenthe, Groningen and Guelders,
very often in the immediate vicinity of an urnfield. These
so-called *Heidense Legerplaatsen* ('heathens' camps') are clearly
related to the British 'Celtic Fields' and the Danish 'Porse-
haver' or 'Oldtidsagre'. They sometimes cover an area of
100–150 acres, divided by a network of low earthen banks
into irregular strips of 4–10 acres. That they are in fact small
fields is proved by traces of old plough-marks, and by agro-
nomic soil analysis. The origin of these earthen levées has been
explained by the fact that the peasants have at certain times
taken off the sterile upper soil layer, and deposited this earth
on their field boundaries. Elsewhere, during the same period,
but even more so later, drainage ditches were used to separate
the fields, and at the same time the fertile soil from these
ditches was spread on the surface of the fields. The date of
these 'heathens' camps' is uncertain; the most one can say is
that they belong to the Iron Age. Some may go back to Hallstatt times—for this reason we have described them here—
others date very probably from La Tène. Lastly should be mentioned the find in Drenthe (Echten, Loom and Sleen) of four
arrow-shaped wooden ard-shares, probably belonging to the
final Bronze Age or the beginnings of the Iron Age.

We will now have to consider the area to the east and to the
south-east of the region occupied by the Hallstatt warriors of
Hainaut and Belgian Brabant. The introduction of the use of
iron in Belgium started a flourishing industry, mainly in the
Entre-Sambre-et-Meuse, Belgian Lorraine and the Liège
regions. This industry probably began in Hallstatt times and
continued during La Tène, the Roman period, the Middle
Ages and later. Rich iron-ore deposits (oligiste, haematite,
limonite, etc.) were indeed to be found in the subsoil of this
area; they were very intensively mined and were worked-out

K

as late as the nineteenth century. The methods of extracting the metal from the iron ore were very primitive, and the iron slag still contained a considerable percentage of metal, even as much as 40%. Consequently enormous heaps of this iron slag, which were given the name of 'Crayats des Sarrasins', were formed on these sites, mainly in the Entre-Sambre-et-Meuse during the Iron Age, the Roman period and the Middle Ages. Calculations show that such a mound at Géronsart (prov. Namur) contained more than 7,000 cubic yards of slag and weighed more than 13,500 tons! During the industrial revolution of the nineteenth century, mainly during the second half, and also during the early twentieth century, this iron slag was re-utilized in the modern blast-furnaces to extract the large quantities of metal which it still contained. In several places, for instance at Roux-les-Fosses, Rochefort and Lustin (prov. Namur), at Verviers (prov. Liège) and at Groenendaal (Brabant), traces of hearth-furnaces were discovered, difficult to date, but some of which certainly are protohistoric (Hallstatt or La Tène), while others belong to the Roman period or to the Early Middle Ages. Lastly, in the marshy areas of Campine was found a rather poor limonite which was also exploited in protohistoric times, namely in the region of Genk.

Small gold nuggets were found in a few rivers in the Ardennes during the prehistoric period. During the Iron Age—a closer date is not possible—an attempt was made to extract the metal by washing. Along the upper reaches of the Amblève and the Lhomme, and elsewhere, numerous heaps of sand, the remains of this industry, have been found. Moreover, it seems that the same technique was still being used in Roman times.

Traces of Hallstatt habitations are known from Furfooz ('Montagne du Châlet') where a calcite quarry existed, and from Hulsonniaux ('Abri de la Poterie') in the valley of the River Lesse.

More important, however, are the Hallstatt remains found in

the extreme south of our regions, in Belgian Lorraine, the province of Luxembourg and the Grand-Duchy of Luxembourg.

In the 'Grand Bois' at Saint-Vincent (Luxembourg), a large barrow-cemetery of more than 120 burials has been excavated. These tumuli, without peripheral structures, had a diameter of 15–35 ft., occasionally 50 ft. The cremated bones were either deposited in an urn or scattered around the grave-goods; elsewhere the barrow was built on top of the funeral pyre; and lastly, in a few cases, the bones were protected by a heap of big stones which was then covered by the mound. The very poor grave-goods included, apart from the funerary urn, a few pieces of pottery and small fragments of iron or bronze (razor, bracelet, pin, torque, fibula, etc.); weapons are lacking. These metal objects suggest a date of final Hallstatt/ early La Tène. If this date is correct, the pottery seems to be rather archaic and closely resembles the vessels of the final Bronze Age Urnfield people: urns with globular body and cylindrical or slightly widening neck, small-handled cups, truncated bowls. This cemetery is clearly related to the Haulzy necropolis, in French Lorraine, dating from the same period; it is in this direction one must look to link up this cemetery with a larger cultural ensemble.

Other remains of the same area, however, are related to the cultures of the Eifel region: the Mehren culture and Hunsrück-Eifel culture (end of Hallstatt and beginning of La Tène). At Aalborg near Beaufort (Grand Duchy of Luxembourg), a large farm has been excavated, dated by the pottery from the middle of the fifth century B.C. The plan is rectangular, 102 by 29 ft.; the post-holes indicate a building with a central nave and two side aisles. The northern part served as living quarters, and was entirely paved with big irregular stones. The southern section was used as a stable; here only the central nave was paved, while the floor of the two side-aisles—perhaps sub-divided into a series of small boxes—consisted of trampled earth. The gable roof was supported by posts separating the nave from the aisles.

Lastly, near the end of the Hallstatt period, people began to settle on and fortify the so-called '*éperons barrés*', which, however, are typical more of La Tène fortifications, and about which more will be said in the next chapter. We will only mention here the *oppidum* of Montauban at Buzenol (Luxembourg), with sheer cliffs on two sides. These natural defences have been strengthened by a rampart, also running along the third side. This rampart consists at the base of large wooden beams, put alternately lengthwise and crosswise, and is capped by a thick layer of stones. The whole construction was burnt—intentionally, according to the excavators—to form a massive vitrified ensemble; after the fire, the outer face of the rampart was strengthened by a wall of dry masonry. A few pottery sherds, some of which are related to the pottery found at the Saint-Vincent cemetery, while others call to mind the ware from the Hunsrück-Eifel culture, suggest a date of final Hallstatt/early La Tène. This *oppidum,* whose rampart was built with a completely different technique from the *murus gallicus* of La Tène times, can certainly be compared with the 'vitrified forts' of the British Isles, Germany, Bohemia and France. These, too, can in a general way be said to belong to the final Hallstatt period. The *oppidum* at Buzenol continued to be occupied during La Tène times, and it is this period which will now be considered.

CHAPTER IX

The End of the Prehistoric Period

BESIDES THE INFORMATION we have obtained from archaeological investigation about the last centuries preceding the Roman conquest, we have the writings of several classical authors on our regions during that period. However, it is not always possible to combine or to bring together both categories of sources. Thus, for instance, Caesar and other authors, taking their knowledge from descriptions probably going back to Posidonius of Apamea, maintain that, in the first century B.C. the Rhine formed the frontier between the two main populations of protohistoric Western Europe, Germans and Gauls. We know, however, from Caesar himself, that the territory of the Gaulish tribe of the Menapii extended along the coast even further north than the Rhine delta (region of Leyden), while on the other hand archaeological evidence shows that the area on both banks of this river south of Cologne belonged to the Hunsrück-Eifel culture. Notwithstanding these facts, it may be said that for a great part the information is correct, and—for the Low Countries—we think it may be correlated with the marked opposition already shown since the Urnfield invasions, between the areas to the south and to the north of this river, opposition which will become even more accentuated during La Tène times. We will first examine the Germanic territory during the La Tène period, to give a description of the Celtic area afterwards.

We have somewhat more detailed information on the northern provinces of the Netherlands for the last four centuries B.C. than for the preceding period. A clear distinction can be made between the sandy areas (South-East Frisia, the south of the province of Groningen, Drenthe, Veluwe, etc.) where we find the descendants of the Urnfield population of the previous centuries—whose main occupation seems to have been agriculture—and the clay area in the north of the provinces of Frisia and Groningen. This last became habitable after the sea-regression of 300 B.C. and was occupied by a new population coming from the east and mainly concerned with stock-breeding. Almost no traces of La Tène civilization are known from the western provinces (Utrecht, South and North Holland), and these regions seem to have been almost unoccupied.

A characteristic common to both cultures is their great material poverty, especially when compared with the area south of the Rhine. Even though we are fully in the Iron Age, iron objects are extremely scarce. Trade with the adjacent regions is practically non-existent, to say nothing of the faraway Mediterranean countries. The use of money, which appears to the south of the Rhine during La Tène II, remains unknown to the north of the river. At the most may be mentioned a few bronze objects indicating trade relations with the Jastorf culture area from northern Germany, the Nieuw-Weerdinge hoard (Drenthe) containing a bronze torque of Late Hallstatt type, two early La Tène bossed bracelets (imported from the South?) and a necklace of fifteen amber beads, and a very fine dagger with iron blade and anthropomorphic bronze handle found at Havelte (Drenthe); it seems to date from La Tène II and is the only important piece found in the Netherlands, north of the Rhine, and imported from the Marne region of the La Tène civilization.

Fig 34

The Urnfield people of the sandy areas did not advance much further westward than the River Ijssel. Their graves are known, as are their fields and some of their habitations. Two types of tombs can be distinguished. In Drenthe (for example, at Zeijen, Balloo, Anlo), side by side with the Urnfield cemeteries, barrows are still being built on top of funeral pyres,

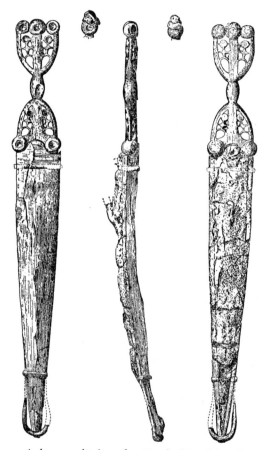

Fig. 34. Anthropomorphic dagger from Havelte (Drenthe). About 1:3.

after the Late Bronze Age native traditions. At Zeijen, the grave-goods of one of these barrows included a La Tène I fibula, while at Balloo two bronze crescent-shaped ear-rings (*Segelohrringe*) were found, typical of the same period. Similar barrows are in use in this area as late as Roman times. The Urnfield cemeteries are quite numerous. The graves have a circular or oval peripheral ditch, while near the end of the period square ditches appear. In two cases (Balloo, Drenthe, and Laudermarke, Groningen), these square ditches are enclosed by a peripheral palisade. The urns are of varied shapes, but the biconical vases have practically disappeared and of the Harpstedt urns only very few examples are found.[1] As during the preceding period, this pottery shows marked affinities with the urns of the same period found in Hanover and Westphalia. The grave-goods are extremely poor, almost non-existent. At the most there may be an occasional small iron object, very often almost completely destroyed by oxidation. At Wijster (Drenthe) an iron pin was discovered together with a bronze fibula, which may be attributed to the Jastorf civilization. Excavation has revealed near the graves in several of these cemeteries—those at Emst (Veluwe), Laudermarke (Groningen), Hijken (Drenthe), for instance—quadrangular or rectangular series of post-holes, suggesting small wooden constructions which have been interpreted at shrines. They may be compared with the similar constructions from the Hallstatt cemetery at Lommel-Kattenbos (Belgian Limburg).[2] Such funerary chapels continued to exist in northern Gaul and the Rhineland in Roman times and even as late as in some Merovingian cemeteries.

In the preceding chapter we have described the traces of prehistoric fields, discovered near a certain number of these cemeteries; it must be remembered that, if some fields belong to the Hallstatt period, others are of La Tène age. At two sites in Drenthe and Groningen respectively, the remains of habitations situated near the fields have been excavated: a small two-roomed rectangular house (21 by 26 ft.) at Sellingen, another of similar type at Peest. The same sandy area has yielded traces of several other habitations (Zeijen, Rhee, Noordbarge in Drenthe, Margijnen Enk in Overijssel, Fochteloo in Frisia, etc.), but dating from the first centuries A.D., and therefore falling outside the limits set for this book.

Since the end of the Boreal phase, the present-day clay zone in the north of the provinces of Frisia and Groningen had been covered by the ocean, and a coastal lagoon was formed where the sea slowly deposited a layer of gradually emerging loamy sedimentation. At the end of the fourth century B.C., the sea covered this land only at exceptionally high tides, and extensive lush meadows of salt-loving grasses appeared, which must have been very temping to a population of herdsmen. Archaeo-logical remains show that the first colonization of the area dates from about 300 B.C. The pottery indicates that these settlers did not come from the sandy zone bordering the new land, but had their origin in northern Germany. They originally settled at meadow-level, but very soon they discovered their precarious and dangerous position. To be safe from flooding and to pro-tect their cattle, they built artificial mounds—known as *terpen* in Frisia and *wierden* in Groningen—out of turf sods. Some of these mounds were relatively small and were used only for one single farm and its outbuildings; others were much larger and covered a surface of sometimes up to forty acres: they were occu-pied by a complete village. Lastly, small uninhabited mounds were used as refuges for cattle in case of flooding. Numerous mounds have been repeatedly heightened when they proved to be too low for exceptionally severe floods: several are as much as 23 ft. above sea-level. The successive habitation levels can easily be distinguished by a thick layer of humus mixed with dung. The archaeological remains, even of organic material (wood, leather, textiles) have been preserved in excellent condi-tion and show an almost complete picture of the material equipment of the *terpen* inhabitants. Such *terpen* have been built all along the coast of the North Sea, from Frisia to Denmark, between 300 B.C. and the eleventh century A.D., at which period a beginning was made with the systematic diking of the low-lying land. From the eleventh century onwards, a number of these mounds were abandoned, and their inhabitants moved to the lower land; others, however, continued to be occupied and even to this day quite a lot of villages in this area are situated on their artificial *terp*. The old centre of the towns of Leeuwarden and Emden have been built on several ancient *terpen*. Because of the organic material it contains, the soil of these mounds is very fertile; for this reason a large number has been flattened in the course of the nineteenth and twentieth centuries, and the soil used for improving the less fertile fields. Originally in the provinces of Frisia and Groningen alone more than a thousand *terpen* must have existed, but more than half of this number have now disappeared.

The *terpen* culture is known by the remains discovered during levelling works and also from systematic excavation. The most important of these are the excavations at Ezinge, north-west of Groningen. Six successive occupation levels have been recognized by A. E. van Giffen, extending from 300 B.C. to the middle of the thirteenth century A.D. Only the three oldest levels fall into the chronological scope of this book. They belong to what P. C. J. A. Boeles has called the proto-Frisian period (300–50 B.C.). During the oldest phase the habitation site was established on ground-level and not yet on an artificial mound. Inside a rectangular enclosure 56 by 85 ft., surrounded by a palisade, were discovered two rectangular houses with a central nave and two side-aisles, built of wooden beams with wattle-and-daub walls. One, completely excavated, was 20 by 43 ft.; the living space, with hearth, was separated by a wattle partition from the cowhouse, with its double row of stalls and central pathway. At right-angles to this farmhouse, a series of post-holes was found forming a rectangle of 27 by 23 ft.: they were probably the traces of a barn built on posts to protect the harvest from damp. The second phase closely followed the first one and can be dated to Middle La Tène times, thanks to the pottery and a bronze pin with U-shaped bend near the top. The second habitation was situated on an artificial mound,

Plate 49

initially 6½ ft. high and approximately 115 ft. in diameter. At least four farms were built close together—probably as an additional protection against gales—whose plan corresponds exactly with the farms of the preceding period; however, no partition was found separating the living quarters from the stables. The length of the buildings varies between 26 and 49 ft. During the third phase, the *terp* was enlarged and heightened by means of a thick layer of organic material; its diameter was then about 330 ft. This rather long phase includes the years preceding, and the beginnings of, the Roman period. The farms—still with the same ground-plan—have been reconstructed several times and they are arranged radially around a small square. The pottery makes a distinction into two sub-periods possible, the first lasting till about 50 B.C. A definite change in the pottery about that time perhaps indicates the arrival of new population elements and marks the end of the proto-Frisian period.

The proto-Frisian *terpen* culture is known not only by the village of Ezinge, but also by excavations and finds from numerous other sites. If we know next to nothing about the graves of this period, the habitations on the contrary yielded a considerable amount of information. It is remarkable that the farms, like the ones at Ezinge, typical of this culture, represent the prototype of the modern Frisian farm, with living-quarters and stables under the same roof. The stables were arranged along a central passage. In these boxes, each for two head of cattle, the cows stood with their heads toward the outer wall after the old Frisian manner still customary at the present day. They stood with the hindlegs on a wattle matting (replaced in more recent days by a broad plank). One of these farmsteads, 23½ ft. wide and at least 79 ft. long, provided stabling for fifty-two cows. This continuity of more than twenty centuries in the plan of the farm buildings alone is enough to justify the name of 'proto-Frisian' given to this civilization, notwithstanding the arrival of newcomers about 50 B.C., that is to say, some thirty-eight years before the classical authors mention the area as being occupied by the Frisians.

Amongst the other remains of this culture—apart from a series of wooden objects, such as a remarkable double yoke found at Ezinge—pottery occurs. The most typical vessels have a lightly incised geometrical decoration (triangles, lozenges, cross-hatching, chevrons, etc.), sometimes filled with a chalky paste made from crushed sea-shells. The oldest forms often have a high neck and small handles or prehension lugs, while the more recent types have a low neck and lack the handles or lugs. Three painted pottery sherds (from Hichtum and Kubaard) probably come from pottery imported from the Rhineland. In the oldest levels at Hichtum and Wommels, a few sherds of Harpstedt-type vessels still occur. Lastly, a few bronze and iron ornaments must be mentioned: bronze torque with geometric decoration, rather like the torques from the Lüne- burg region, bronze spiral brooch and bronze *châtelaine* found in the *terp* at Zwichum, a few glass-paste beads, pins with U- shaped bend near the top (an iron one from Achlum, a bronze one from Ezinge) indicative of trade relations with the Jastorf civilization, and last of all a number of La Tène type fibulae, especially from *terpen* along the River Hunze (Groningen).

The plan of the farms (similar buildings of the same period are known from the area of the Weser and the Elbe) and the pottery with geometrical decoration (calling to mind pottery from the regions of Kassel, Fulda and Berlin) indicate that the origin of this proto-Frisian culture must be sought in northern Germany.

The two groups of Germanic peoples which we find north of the Rhine during the La Tène period, had a markedly peaceful character; they did not participate in the mainly south- ward Germanic expansion which took place at that time on the right bank of the river. These peoples probably still lived in a so-called pre-ethnic phase—that is to say, they had not yet reached the stage of politically organized tribes—as has been shown by a recent study of G. Walser. This situation changes around the middle of the first century B.C., and we shall have to revert to the problem at the end of the present chapter.

Let us now consider the Celtic territory south of the River Rhine. To describe in detail the history of the Celtic expansion is not possible in a book of this size. Suffice it to say that there are very good reasons to admit that the arrival of the Celts in the area under consideration coincides with the Late Bronze Age immigration of the Lower Rhine Urnfield people. We have already insisted on the peaceful character of these poor farmers and herdsmen; this is in marked contrast with the warrior tribes living in the area that may be considered as the Celtic cradle: Upper and Middle Rhine, and north-eastern France. There a powerful warrior aristocracy ruled, under whose impulse the Celtic tribes of this region started a series of military operations, already as early as the Hallstatt period. They were directed, now against other Celtic tribes—a typical example is the conquest of Hainaut and Brabant by the Hallstatt warriors, described in the preceding chapter, now against more distant lands. These expeditions became very frequent during the fifth and fourth centuries, and ended with the submission to the Celts of vast territories comprising England, the largest part of France, northern Spain and Italy, southern Germany, Bohemia, the Balkans and even part of Asia Minor. On the other hand, the trade relations between the Mediterranean lands and the Celtic world played an ever-increasing part during Hallstatt times. Via Marseilles and the Rhône valley, but mainly by way of the passes through the Alps—Great St Bernard, Brenner— numerous Mediterranean products, Italic and Etruscan bronzes, Greek pottery and jewels, arrived in Central and Western Europe, where they are found in the very rich 'princes' tombs' of the Celtic aristocracy. The Oss-grave already described is but a poor example compared with the lavish display of the tomb at Vix (Côte d'Or), dating from the final Hallstatt. Under these Mediterranean influences, combined with the ani-mal style of the Scythians—with whom the Celts had come in contact along the Danube and in the Balkans—a new civiliza-tion developed during the fifth century B.C. in the area which saw the origins of the Celtic world. In many aspects this new culture is but a continuation of the Hallstatt civilization, but with a very original and characteristic art. This ornamental art, as is seen in the jewellery, ornaments, toilet articles, weapons, etc., amalgamated into a single exuberant and baroque whole —typical of the Celtic mind—floral and plant elements (palmette, lotus) borrowed from the Greeks, zoomorphic ele-ments of Scythian origin and anthropomorphic designs. This La Tène civilization dominated the whole of Central and Western Europe till the Roman conquest. We find it in our own regions south of the Rhine, but in a very attenuated form. Indeed, as during the preceding periods, the inhabitants of the Low Countries were mainly poorish farmers, and the ruling aristocracy did not play the same role here as it did among the more southerly Celtic tribes. Archaeological investigation has discovered only relatively few traces of this aristocracy, much poorer and less influential than in the Marne, the Champagne, Burgundy and the Upper and Middle Rhine. This explains why the inhabitants of our regions had no part in the Celtic expansion during the La Tène period. Again, when from the third century B.C. onwards, the decline of the Celtic world started—due to the southward advance of the Germans and the defeats of the Celts in Italy and in Asia Minor—the repercus-sions of these changes had but little influence on the Low Countries. However, before enumerating the events that pre-ceded the Roman conquest, the archaeological remains of the La Tène period must be described. This material is generally rather poor, and no clear differentiation into La Tène I (450–300), La Tène II (300–100) and La Tène III (100–Roman conquest) can be made, as is possible in north-eastern France, where it is based upon the typological evolution of weapons and other objects. In most cases, a distinction can be made only between Early and Late La Tène.

There is no uniformity in the La Tène civilization of our regions, and at least three local groups can be distinguished. The first is to be found in the southern provinces of the Nether-lands (south part of Guelders, Limburg, North Brabant), the sandy area of northern Belgium (Campine, Flanders) and, next to it, the northern part of Belgian Brabant and Hesbaye. A second group is localized in Hainaut, and is more closely related to the Marne and Aisne civilization. Lastly, east of the Sambre-Meuse valley, mainly in highland Belgium, a third group exists whose culture is rather similar to the Moselle and Hunsrück-Eifel culture.

The remains of the first group comprise cemeteries and habi-tation sites. The cemeteries are less numerous than during the preceding period, but the tomb structure and the funeral ritual show a marked continuity with the Late Bronze Age and Hallstatt urnfields. Cremation is still exclusively practised. Either the bones are deposited in an urn, or part of the bones and charcoal from the pyre are scattered around it; sometimes the tomb is built over the pyre itself, or lastly, the burnt bones can also be buried without an urn. Barrows are still rather numerous, but more and more flat graves become the rule. Sometimes, the barrows have no peripheral ditch (Lommel Kattenbos), sometimes such a ditch exists and may, in some cases, be interrupted (as at Strijbeek); the grave-mounds have a tendency to become smaller than in Hallstatt times. The grave-goods are very poor and include, apart from the cinerary urn, an occasional accessory vessel or a metal object (belt hook, iron ring, button, etc.). The pottery is very typical and shows that the 'Marnian' style has penetrated even to these northern Celtic areas. Indeed, in Early La Tène times a start was made in the Marne and Aisne region with the fabrication of a characteristic sort of pottery, with carinated body and angu⁄ lar profile, showing clearly that a transposition of metal forms into ceramics was intended. It is not impossible that some very finely made vases were imported directly from the Marne, with carinated body and slightly widening neck, decorated with geometric motifs resembling Greek meanders, like the beautiful examples found at Gentbrugge (East Flanders), Rijkevorsel (prov. Antwerp), Lommel (Belgian Limburg),

Plates 53, 54

etc. But, apart from vases of Hallstatt tradition, what is mainly found in the cemeteries is a local imitation of Marnian pottery, often badly baked and rather coarsely made: urns with angu⁄ lar profile, big carinated bowls, etc. Amongst the more im⁄ portant cemeteries where such pottery has been found are Wijchen (Guelders), Elsloo, Caberg, Posterholt and Weert (Dutch Limburg), Baarle⁄Nassau, Alphen, Riel, Strijbeek and Bergeik (North Brabant), Lommel and Ophoven (Bel⁄ gian Limburg) and Rijkevorsel (prov. Antwerp). At Ber⁄ geik and Elsloo a few painted pottery sherds, probably imported from the Rhineland, were discovered. Most of these cemeteries were continuously occupied up to Roman times. During Late La Tène, the pottery becomes less angular, some vases have a rudimentary circular foot, and several bowls and urns are decorated with a comb⁄decoration consisting of a series of narrow parallel lines.

One single tomb, discovered at Eigenbilzen (Belgian Lim⁄ burg) in 1871, was exceptionally rich for our regions. The grave⁄goods of this 'prince's tomb' consisted of a bronze

Plate 52
Plate 51

cordoned bucket imported from northern Italy and containing the cremated bones, a bronze oenochoe with trilobate beak, finely decorated with floral and animal motifs (volutes, pal⁄ mettes, griffons) and imported from Etruria, fragments of a second bronze oenochoe with biconical body engraved with geometric ornaments, a thin band in gold leaf with *à-jour* decoration of floral motifs executed in purely Celtic style and originally fixed to one of the oenochoes, a fragment of a bronze ring covered with gold leaf, and unidentifiable pieces of iron. This extremely rich ensemble may be dated from about 400 B.C.

Plate 56

The trade with distant lands as shown by the Eigenbilzen burial, is also illustrated by two other finds from the same region. A superb silver disc was discovered at Helden (Dutch Limburg), with a decoration in relief showing, in the centre of a frieze of fantastic beasts, the battle of a man with an animal. This object, the style of which is closely related to another disc in Paris and to the famous Gundestrup cauldron, probably dates from about 100 B.C., and it has almost certainly been imported from the eastern Celtic lands; Scythian influences are very apparent. A beautiful bronze mirror, with engraved and enamelled volute decoration, found at Nijmegen, seems to have come from England and probably dates from the first century A.D. Notwithstanding its purely Celtic character, it therefore falls outside the chronological limits of this book.[3]

Plate 57

The habitation sites are scarce in the sandy area of the southern part of the Netherlands and Campine. The hut-traces found at Lommel-Hoever Heide (cf. *supra*), dating from final Hallstatt to Early La Tène may be mentioned. At Genk remains have been discovered of an iron industry based on the limonite of the marshlands. Habitation sites are more numerous in the region to the south of this sandy area, near Malines and Louvain on one hand, in Hesbaye on the other. The only known cemetery from the Malines-Louvain area is the one from Aarschot-Langdorp, already occupied during the Hallstatt period, but with a few La Tène burials. The most satisfactorily excavated habitation site is from Malines-Nekkerspoel. In the centre of a lake, on a small artificial isle made of branches and earth, the remains of about five rectangular houses were discovered. The angular pottery with Marnian influences suggests a date of Early La Tène. The most spectacular find was a canoe 27½ ft. long, dug out of an oak trunk by means of iron tools. The inhabitants were cattle-breeders, as is shown by the numerous bones of ox, pig, goat and horse. The site was destroyed by fire, and the skeletons of several unfortunate individuals who perished in the catastrophe, were discovered. At Rumst, a few miles to the north of Malines, were found the traces of a circular hut, half dug into the soil, and with two successive occupation levels. The first yielded but few material remains and seems to date from final Hallstatt or Early La Tène times, while the second may be attributed to Middle and Late La Tène, thanks to its carinated Marnian-type pottery and several comb-decorated sherds. Amongst the finds are a curious pottery sieve, a loom-weight, parts of a grinding stone and even a fragment of a polished stone axe. In the near-by village of Duffel was found a beautiful iron chimney-crook of the La Tène III period, which may be compared with a similar piece from Anderlecht, near Brussels. More to the east, an important site was excavated, unfortunately rather sketchily, at the Kessel-berg near Louvain. Only the pottery sherds and a few other objects were kept. Fragments of wattle-and-daub walling are the only indications of dwellings. Apart from loom-weights, fragments of grinding-stones and pieces of polished stone axes, pottery was found closely resembling the ware from the Campine cemeteries, and dating from the whole of the La Tène period. Next to Marnian-type pots, a few other sherds of more coarse aspect were observed, possibly deriving from the Hilversum/Drakenstein/Harpstedt tradition. Only few La Tène remains are known from Hesbaye. Very angular pottery of Marnian type was discovered on a few badly excavated hut-sites of which no plan exists at Omal and Moxhe (prov. Liège). In the same region, at Jandrain-Jandrenouille (Brabant), another La Tène habitation site was recently excavated, but no details have so far been published. A little more to the north, at Tongres, a bronze La Tène I helmet was found, originally decorated with an ornamental band which has now disappeared.

The area to the west of the River Scheldt, Flanders, has not yielded many more traces of the civilization of the last centuries B.C. At Waasmunster-Zombeke, a habitation site was des-troyed by mechanical excavation, and only the sherds of a few pots of Marnian tradition were recovered. The beautiful Marnian vessel from Gentbrugge has already been mentioned. Plate 54 From the immediate vicinity of the Hallstatt cemetery at Aalter, a new surface finds of sherds resembling the pottery from La Panne are known, indicating that the site continued to be occu-pied during La Tène times. A new lake-village was built during the Iron Age in the marshy valley of the River Mandel, south of the site where from the Neolithic to the Late Bronze Age the lake-dwelling of Dentergem was situated. Big posts were driven into the marshy soil and connected with transverse beams, carrying a platform of thinner tree-trunks on top of which the houses were built. This village was occupied during the whole of the Roman period and even as late as the Middle Ages; the Iron Age remains are very scarce and consist of a few sherds only. The only site in Flanders which is a little better known is La Panne. In the immediate vicinity of the sea a small settlement existed, composed of farms, one of which measured 20 by 13 ft. Food remains indicate that the inhabi-tants practised agriculture, cattle-breeding (ox, sheep, goat, pig, horse), fishing, and occasionally hunted red deer, fox and hare. Amongst them a certain number of salt-makers must be reckoned, who extracted salt from sea-water by boiling; this is proved by the existence of numerous hearths and traces of briquetage (clay bars), identical to the briquetage found in the famous Essex Red Hills. Several clay loom-weights were dis-covered, together with spinning whorls, fibulae, iron imple-ments and numerous pottery sherds, indicating that the site

Plate 60
Plate 61

was occupied from Early La Tène till well into the Roman period. A few pots with angular profile go back to Early La Tène; in Late La Tène times the typical shapes become more rounded and several pots have a comb, or a cardium-decoration. Others are covered with irregular cross-hatching, while the outer wall of several big storage-jars is entirely decorated with fingertip impressions. A few cremation burials have also been found; the bones were sometimes deposited in an urn, or more often buried without any grave-goods at all.

A more prosperous culture is found in Hainaut, the area of the second group. This culture seems to be related to the Marne and Aisne civilization, apart from a few rather important differences (like the cremation ritual; for in the Marne area only inhumation was practised during Early La Tène). The Leval-Trahegnies cemetery, unfortunately completely disturbed and badly excavated, comprised relatively rich graves dating from La Tène I to La Tène III. The oldest pottery includes high carinated urns with the neck sometimes decorated with geometric patterns, and carinated bowls. In Late La Tène times the forms are heavier and more rounded. Curious pots completely covered with small pyramidal knobs are also found, probably dating from the third or second century B.C. A La Tène II woman's tomb contained a superb bronze chain-belt, a hook decorated with red enamel, and two lignite bracelets. This is one of the oldest enamelled objects from our regions. On the evidence of the classical authors, bronze enamelling was a Celtic invention; it knew considerable industrial development during the Roman period, especially in Belgium. A man's grave has yielded a beautiful La Tène II sword, still in its iron sheath. Lastly, the cemetery contained at least two chariot-burials, one from La Tène I, the other from La Tène III.[4] The oldest yielded axe-pins in enamelled bronze, decorated with the head of a fantastic animal, while the finds of the other one include a tin-coated bronze yoke-ring (the tinning of bronze was equally a Celtic invention), and other pieces of the chariot and horse-trappings in enamelled bronze. The Mont Eribus cemetery, near Mons, although poorer, also belongs to the same civilization, as is shown by the pottery; the grave-goods contained several fibulae. This cemetery was also occu-pied during the whole of the La Tène period. A rather dif-ferent sort of pottery appears during Late La Tène, comprising small, very coarsely made pots rather like some Late La Tène vessels from the Middle Rhine. It must also be mentioned that in the Mont Eribus cemetery the only example known in our regions of a prehistoric wheel-turned vase was discovered. While the use of the pottery-wheel was known in Germany and France during the Iron Age, it was not introduced in the Low Countries until Roman times. Two graves discovered at Ciply, in the centre of the Merovingian cemetery of the 'Champ des Agaises', belong to the same group. Each of the two crema-tion burials contained an iron knife, together with pottery. In the first grave were found four pottery vessels, two skulls of wild boar and numerous snail shells. To the same group also belong several isolated finds from Thuillies (spear-head), Epinois and Harmignies (pottery), and Chapelle-lez-Herlai-mont. In this last village, at a place called 'le Chauffour' were discovered two ram-headed firedogs in baked clay, of a type which occurs frequently in the Celtic area in France, and which prove the existence in Hainaut of the Gallic cult of the hearth. These objects probably date from the first half of the first cen-tury B.C. Lastly, a brief description must be given of the superb treasure found in 1861 at Frasnes-lez-Buissenal. A pot-tery vase contained about fifty Gallic electrum coins and two gold torques. The largest one, with a diameter of nearly 8 in., is superbly decorated with zoomorphic ornaments, classified by P. Jacobsthal under his 'plastic style'; it is made of a gold leaf (88% gold + 10% silver) mounted on a core consisting of iron, resin and wax. The second torque is simpler and its metal

Plate 62

Plate 55

Plate 59

Plate 58

is not so pure (65% gold + 35% silver and copper), the diameter is 4¾ in. The two pieces probably date from the second
century B.C., but the coins have probably been struck between
75 and 50 B.C. For this reason the suggestion that the treasure
was buried at the moment of the Roman invasion, is not at all
improbable.

This leaves the regions to the east of the Sambre-Meuse
valley to be described. We need do no more than mention here
once again the remains of the iron industry from the Entre-
Sambre-et-Meuse and the Liège regions, and the extraction of
gold along certain rivers in the Ardennes; both have already
been dealt with in the preceding chapter.

Amongst the most impressive remains of this area are a
series of *oppida,* fortified hills of the *éperon barré* type. These
heights are bordered on three sides by sheer cliffs, the fourth
side being a gentle slope. In some cases only this fourth side
has been fortified, while in others the cliffs also have been included in a peripheral enclosure. Some of these forts go back
to Late Hallstatt times, as has already been shown, but most
of them seem to date from the La Tène period. However, only
a few have been satisfactorily excavated, and even where more
detailed investigations have been made, the finds of pottery,
weapons and tools are often too scarce to allow a very precise
dating. It is impossible to record here all these *oppida.* The most
important are the ones at 'le Boubier' at Châtelet, the 'Hastedon'
at Saint-Servais, the Mont-Falhize near Huy, Ehein, Olloy,
'Hauterecenne' at Furfooz, Eprave, 'Til-Château' at Hotton,
Bérisménil, Salm-Château, 'Montauban' at Buzenol, the
'Parett' at Nothomb, and the 'Titelberg' at Pétange (Grand
Duchy of Luxembourg). At Montauban, the ramparts were
of the 'vitrified fort' type (cf. *supra*); elsewhere, as at Olloy and
Hastedon, they were built in the *murus gallicus* technique, as
described by Caesar: a series of closely spaced, regular beams
put lengthwise and crosswise following the wall, formed the

core of the ramparts. The interstices between the beams were filled in with stones and earth and the front was covered with a revetment wall in dry-masonry facing. The *oppidum* at Hastedon covered a surface of about thirty-two acres and had an almost pentagonal shape; on four sides it is protected by sheer cliffs 115–130 ft. high, while the fifth side forms a sort of isthmus, 260 ft. wide, connecting the plateau with the adjoining slopes. The cliffs are surmounted by a rampart built in the *murus gallicus* technique, 23 ft. wide and about 1,422 yards long. The isthmus was protected by an earth rampart, $6\frac{1}{2}$ ft. high and 62 ft. wide at the base and 52 ft. at the top; a strong palisade of thick wooden posts was erected on top of this rampart. Lastly, in front of this *vallum* was dug a wide and deep ditch. Definite traces of fire seem to indicate that this *oppidum* was stormed and taken after bitter fighting; it is suggested that the fortress at Hastedon is the *oppidum Atuatucorum,* besieged and captured by Caesar in 57 B.C. It has not been possible to determine whether some of these *oppida* were permanently occupied, or if they were single refuges in time of war. At the Titelberg, however, a considerable amount of coins from the Leuci, Mediomatrici, Remi, Treveri, Suessiones, etc. were discovered, and it seems that this *oppidum* at least was a very much visited market-place. These fortifications, which continue into Germany, were per- haps erected to oppose the Germanic advance to the South on the right bank of the Rhine.

Unlike in the other regions of the Low Countries, inhuma- tion was practised in the area east of the Meuse during La Tène times. Two separate groups can be distinguished in the graves of this period. The first is situated on the heights surrounding the Famenne depression. The tombs are cairns (*marchets*) of late neolithic tradition. It is possible that the inhumation ritual was introduced under the influence of the Ardennes group—about which more will be said later—but the grave- goods rather seem to indicate a relationship with the La Tène civilization of Hainaut. A number of cairns was found in the Han-sur-Lesse area; in one of them the deceased was buried with, on his head, as a crown, a bronze torque—a rite which is also found to have been practised in the Marne region. Other tombs (for example at Silenrieux and Fontenelle) contained pottery closely resembling the Hainaut Early La Tène vases. The second group is localized in the Ardennes properly speaking, in the area of Neufchâteau and Bastogne (Sibret, Wideumont, Juseret, Hamipré, Nivelet, Hollange, Bovigny, Chérain-Sterpigny, Mont-le-Ban, etc.). The dead were buried in rectangular pits, in the corners of which post-holes are sometimes found, traces of a small temporary structure, probably with a ritual significance (mortuary houses?). An earthen tumulus was erected on top of these graves. The grave-goods comprise a few pieces of jewellery and ornaments (bronze bracelets, torsaded torques, ear-rings, sometimes a fibula, like the superb bird-fibula from a tomb at Nivelet), sometimes a weapon and pottery. This last is not of Marnian tradition, but is clearly related to the vases from the Moselle valley and to the Huns-rück-Eifel civilization.

Such is the archaeological material of the three cultural groups which can be distinguished in our regions south of the Rhine. In the area of the first group—the largest one—this material shows a continuity in occupation since Hallstatt times, which indicates that the repercussions of the events of the last centuries B.C. had but little effect upon the Low Countries. La Tène influences were thus relatively feeble and trade relations with the South not intensive. The aristocracy, which did not have the power nor the influence which it possessed amongst the more southerly tribes, nevertheless succeeded in attracting salesmen of Mediterranean goods. When, during La Tène II, the Celts started coining money, the tribes occupying this region—except the Menapii, who lived in Flanders—started doing the same thing, which indicates that

this innovation corresponded with a definite economic necessity. The monetary finds are nevertheless much scarcer than in
the area of the two other groups. The majority of the inhabitants of this first region consisted of not very developed, peaceful
farmers and herdsmen. The classical authors ascribe to the
Celts important advances in agricultural technique: invention
of the heavy wheel-plough with plough-share and mould-
board, use of silos, improving the soil by addition of marl and
chalk, etc. No traces of these innovations have up to now been
discovered in our regions, but this does not mean that they
may not have been well known to our ancestors; the wheel-
plough, capable of opening up the heavy clay lands, was introduced into England by the Belgae during the first century B.C.

In the Hainaut group, on the other hand, we find a much
more sophisticated culture, very closely related to the Marne
and Aisne civilization; its Celtic character is much more pronounced than anywhere else. Its relative richness indicates that
the aristocracy certainly played a more important part here
than was the case in the area situated farther north; this fact is
confirmed by Caesar, where he describes the Nervii living in
this region. On the other hand, Caesar also says that the Nervii
were known for their austere morals, and that they carefully
avoided all contact with the salesmen of Mediterranean goods.
However, archaeological investigation does not prove him right.

Lastly, in the Ardennes, where the change from cremation to
inhumation perhaps indicates the arrival of new population
elements, and where the presence of the *oppida* gives a rather
warrior-like aspect to the La Tène period, the culture is clearly
related to the Hunsrück-Eifel civilization of western Germany.

Only the last events, which mark the end of the prehistoric
period in the Low Countries, remain to be described. The
southward expansion of the Germanic peoples—which can be

followed by archaeology—continued on the right bank of the Rhine during the whole of the La Tène period. It was considerably less important in a westerly direction: we have already insisted upon the peaceful character of the Germanic inhabitants of the northern and eastern provinces of the Netherlands, north of the River Rhine. They did not advance much further to the west than the River Ijssel, so that the north-western provinces of the Netherlands remained practically unoccupied. This state of affairs only changed with the Roman conquest: at the same time, when new population elements appeared in the *terpen* culture of Frisia and Groningen, other Germanic tribes —the Tencteri and the Usipetes—ousted from their own lands in Germany by the Suebi, invaded the transrhenish territories, in the Leyden area, along the coast, occupied by the Gaulish Menapii, only to cross the Rhine and be massacred in Gaul by Caesar.

During their advance towards the South, the Germans gradually pushed back the Celtic tribes established on the right bank of the Rhine. Already during the third century B.C., a group of transrhenish Celts, forced to flee before the German advance, crossed the river and occupied the Moselle valley where they became mixed with the older native population to form the Treveri tribe. Perhaps a connection can be seen between this immigration and the change in population which we have suggested for the Ardennes. Another group of transrhenish Celts, also driven out of their territory by the Germanic advance, crossed the Rhine one century later. These are the Belgae, who can be followed by archaeology in their westward move south of the Ardennes massif, and who established themselves in northern France, between the River Seine and the Ardennes. Although they borrowed a certain number of elements from the older Marnian civilization, archaeological indications—for example, the change from inhumation to cremation, the introduction of new pottery types—show very clearly the arrival of this new population. Their transrhenish origin explains why Caesar attributed to the Belgae a mixed Germanic-Celtic character. He calls 'Belgae' all the peoples living between the Rivers Seine, Marne and Rhine, but the name has here been wrongly used. The migration of the actual Belgae did not pass through the present-day territory of Belgium, where the native population received the name of 'Belgae' only because of Caesar's terminological inaccuracy. The Nervii are the only tribe occupying our regions, who claimed a transrhenish origin, but the archaeological finds from Hainaut do not bear this out. The appearance during Late La Tène of a new type of pottery in the Mont Eribus cemetery (cf. *supra*), is too feeble an indication to suggest the arrival of a new population group. The true Belgian tribes are the Remi, the Catuvellauni, the Suessiones, the Bellovaci, the Veliocasses, the Caleti, the Ambiani, the Viromandui and the Atrebates of northern France.

Towards the end of the second century B.C., the Germanic invasion of the Cimbri and the Teutones took place, an invasion which was only opposed seriously—according to tradition —by the Belgae. The rearguard of these invaders, about 6,000 men, settled in our country and the Atuatuci, who at the time of the Roman conquest occupied the Namur area, were their descendants. Unfortunately, the prehistorical remains, the *oppida* excepted, are very poor in this region, so that archaeology can give no definite indications of them.

At the moment when, in 57 B.C., Caesar appeared in northern Gaul, the following tribes occupied our regions. Along the coast, in north-western France around Boulogne, lived the Morini, whose territory extended to the north as far as the River Aa or perhaps the River Yser. In the latter case, the La Panne settlement may belong to them. If not, it must be attributed to the Menapii, living between the coast and the River Scheldt, whose main branch at the time was the Striene, flowing into the River Meuse. Their territory extended even farther north than the mouth of the Rhine, in the region of Leyden. The Menapii were not very numerous, which explains the scarcity of archaeological finds from this area. Rather backward, they were the only Celtic tribe who did not know coined money. More to the east lived the Nervii and a number of smaller subject tribes, the Centrones, Gedumnii, Grudii, Pleumocii, and Levaci, between the River Scheldt to the west, the Arrouaise forest and the Thiérache to the south, the 'Carbonnaria' forest to the east and the Rivers Rupel and Dyle to the north. Our Hainaut group belongs to this Nervian territory, together with a number of habitation sites of a more backward type which we have mentioned, in the Malines area. It is in the land of the Nervii that the richest and most typical remains of the La Tène civilization of the Low Countries were found. Much larger was the area ocupied by the Eburones, bordering to the west on the territories of the Nervii and the Menapii, delimited in the north and east by the Rhine and in the south by the Ardennes forest (the largest forest in the whole of Gaul, if one can believe Caesar). In this area also lived a few smaller tribes, subject to the Eburones: Segni, Condrusi, Paemani, Caerosi. The Eburones themselves had to pay tribute to the Atuatuci living in the Namur region. It is precisely in the territory of the Eburones that the continuity in population and civilization since Hallstatt times is most marked. Caesar mentions that the Eburones and their subject tribes were sometimes known under the collective name of Germani. This again may only mean a transrhenish origin, but in this case, it must go back as far as Early Hallstatt times or even to the Urnfield invasions. Lastly, in the Ardennes forest and in the Moselle valley lived the Treveri, who have already been mentioned.

Caesar insisted on the rather rough and uncivilized character of the populations of our regions, and this has been confirmed by archaeology. It would therefore be wrong to apply to the Low Countries the information given by the classical authors about the customs, the social organization or the religion of the Celts, and we will not dwell upon these data, which are much more relevant to the prehistory of France than of our own area.

In 57 B.C., Caesar started his conquest of the tribes then living in our land as far north as the Rhine; these different campaigns and battles are not the concern of this book. Large tracts of land, like the territory of the Eburones, were systematically depopulated. For this reason, other transrhenish tribes— for the most part Germanic—established themselves in the land of the Eburones, during the reign of Augustus and with the approval of the Romans. The name of the Eburones disappears from history. These new tribes are the Ubii and Cugerni on the left bank of the Rhine, the Tungri in central Belgium, the Toxandri in Campine and the south of the Netherlands, etc. At about the same time, and probably as a result of the migrations north of the Rhine already mentioned, the Germanic peoples living in the Netherlands appear to be divided into tribes: Batavi, Canninefates, Marsaci, Frisii, etc. In 12 B.C. Drusus started his campaigns with a view to conquering Germany, and in due course the transrhenish provinces of the Netherlands became Roman. They remained under Roman rule until the reign of Claudius, when the Romans definitely withdrew behind the frontier of the Lower Rhine.

The conquests of Caesar and Drusus mark the end of the prehistoric period in the Low Countries. From now on, under Roman rule and very rapidly almost completely romanized— at least south of the Rhine—they definitely enter into History.

Notes

[1] It has been suggested that the eoliths found at Boncelles, near Liège (Belgium), and in the Veluwe (the Netherlands), go back to the beginning of the Pleistocene or even to Tertiary times. Nowadays, however, it is generally admitted that these specimens are not products of human industry, but that the 'retouches' are due to natural causes.

[2] It may be noted that on these sites, the Clactonian and the Acheulean have been found together in the same gravels; the flakes have been separated from the hand-axes on a purely typological basis. Certain arguments, however, plead in favour of a time-separation of these two industries. The whole of the industry has been designated 'Mesvinian' by the first excavators. Since the studies of Breuil, most archaeologists admit a separation between the Clactonian and the Acheulean implements. They maintain the name 'Mesvinian' for the transitional series between the Clactonian and the Levalloiso-Mousterian, to be discussed later. Nevertheless, Spiennes and Mesvin pose the problem of the transition between the flake and hand-axe industries. For that reason alone, these sites merit complete reinvestigation.

[3] In Belgium they are found in the provinces of Hainaut, Brabant and Liège. They are extremely scarce in the Netherlands, because the Riss glaciation has completely changed the aspect of the older deposits. Acheulean bifaces are known from Rijckholt-Sint-Geertruid (Limburg) and from Wijnjeterp (Frisia). The two bifaces from Bathmen (Overijssel), now in the British Museum, are rather suspect. As regards the finds from Wezep (Guelders), Oldebroek (Guelders) and Vollenhove (Overijssel), which have sometimes been interpreted respectively as younger Clactonian, Acheulean and Levalloisian, it is doubtful whether they are artefacts at all!

[4] This industry is traditionally designated as 'Levallois'. We will not use this name, because 'Levallois' can only have a technical, and not a phyletic meaning, as has been proved again by recent studies. The 'Levallois' is in fact an older Mousterian.

CHAPTER II

[1] In fact, not one fossil can be assigned with certainty to the Upper Palaeolithic. Recent studies have proved that the Hengelo skull (Netherlands) is mesolithic, and does not date from the Upper Palaeolithic. The same applies to the two fragments of *radius* from the Martinrive cave (prov. Liège, Belgium). The age of the first Engis skull, thought to be of a Combe-Capelle individual, has been much discussed.

[2] The Solutrean is not represented in the Low Countries. The most one can say is that a few protosolutrean artefacts have been found on the surface, or in clearly Aurignacian levels (Spy, Goyet, Couvin).

[3] The surface deposits from the Belgian Campine (Zonhoven, Zolder, Lommel), attributed by several archaeologists, on a purely typological basis, to the Aurignacian, belong to the Mesolithic and are part of the 'Tjonger'-group (cf. *infra*).

[4] Van Giffen has, with reason, denounced the suspect nature of certain finds made at Elspeet (Veluwe) and in Frisia in the Kuinre valley (Oosterwolde, Prandinge, Makkinga).

CHAPTER III

[1] It must be noted that certain German archaeologists suggest placing some Frisian sites (Donkerbroek, Kjellingen, Prandinge) into the Rissen group.

[2] It would be wrong, however, to say that a site is mesolithic because it contains artefacts in Wommersom quartzite. This material had already been used in middle palaeolithic times (e.g. artefacts found at Fond-de-Forêt), and will be used again in the Neolithic. But it has been in use mainly in mesolithic times.

CHAPTER IV

[1] Radiocarbon tests on the pre-pottery neolithic levels from Jericho indicate that the earliest Neolithic in Palestine dates back to before 6000 B.C.

[2] This rather revolutionary date (the Omalian was traditionally thought to belong to the middle of the third millennium, approximately between 2600 and 2300 B.C.) is based upon recent radiocarbon readings from the Dutch sites of Geleen and Sittard; it has been confirmed by other radiocarbon readings from German Danubian sites.

CHAPTER V

[1] Together with the very vague name of 'polished stone axes—neolithic', the mistaken and now completely out-of-date term of 'Robenhausian' has also frequently been used.

[2] Radiocarbon readings from the megalithic tomb at Diever give a date of 1896±150 B.C.

CHAPTER VI

[1] Only isolated finds are reported from Belgium, where the Beaker civilizations are represented in two areas: the Temse-Termonde region (bell-beakers) and the Campine (mainly Limburg: bell-beakers with ornamentation borrowed from the corded-ware and one corded beaker of late type). This is confirmed by the distribution area of the battle-axes (which, however, do not necessarily belong to these civilizations), although this is larger.

[2] In Belgium, however, sherds of what might be a pot-beaker have been found in the Abri des Aulnes, at Dave (prov. Namur), well to the south of the Beaker area.

[3] The SOM civilization in Belgium can be approximately dated by a very few elements only. The presence of Grand Pressigny blades in the SOM culture as well as in the Dutch Bell-beaker civilization, indicates that both cultures belong approximately to the same period. The Horgen civilization from Switzerland (contemporaneous with the older SOM) is stratigraphically younger than are the Cortaillod and Michelsberg cultures, but older than the Corded-ware civilization. In western Germany, the gallery-graves of the Lippe valley seem to be contemporaneous with the Beaker civilization, while in Sweden the Skogsbo-type gallery-graves appear only in the late Neolithic (Scandinavian chronology) and are therefore later than the older phase of the *Båtyxkultur*.

M

CHAPTER VII

[1] Until recently, the Hilversum/Drakenstein urns were known under the name of Deverel/Rimbury urns, and dated from the end of the Bronze Age. They were thought to be related to the English Deverel/Rimbury urns (which are later by at least some centuries), and an invasion of England by people from the Low Countries was suggested. Recent studies by W. Glasbergen have shown that this interpretation of the facts is not correct.

[2] The Late Bronze Age is frequently designated by Dutch archaeologists as Montelius IV, V and VI, while in Belgium the term mostly employed is Hallstatt A/B. Because the name 'Hallstatt' evokes the first Iron Age (which in the Low Countries starts only with Hallstatt C), we will follow the Dutch terminology, which also makes possible a more precise chronological division.

[3] They used both the rivers and the land routes. Timber trackways, as already known from the late Neolithic (*supra*), were still being built during the Bronze Age: the one at Haaksbergen (Overijssel) has been dated palynologically from the Subboreal.

CHAPTER IX

[1] These vessels, which probably derive from the Hilversum/Drakenstein urns (cf. *supra*), have also been discovered in the oldest levels of some North/Frisian *terpen*, and pottery of the same tradition is known from a number of La Tène habitation sites in Belgium.

[2] With the difference that north of the Rhine these shrines have no peripheral ditch—which, on the contrary, exists around the tombs. Whereas at Lommel exactly the opposite is true: graves without, but cult buildings with, circular ditch!

[3] A silver vase of Greek origin was discovered at Neerharen (Belg. Limburg). It is sometimes dated from Late La Tène times, but belongs more probably to the beginnings of the Roman period.

[4] A not yet published chariot/burial was also discovered near Nijmegen.

Short Bibliography
General Works

J. H. HOLWERDA, *Nederland's Vroegste Geschiedenis,* Amsterdam, 1925.

A. W. BIJVANCK, *De Voorgeschiedenis van Nederland,* Leiden, 1946.

C. C. W. J. HIJSZELER, *Voorgeschiedenis van Nederland* (in: G. S. A. MULDERS, *Handboek der Geografie van Nederland,* II, pp. 188-267) Zwolle, 1951.

E. SACCASYN DELLA SANTA, *La Belgique préhistorique,* Brussels, 1946.

M. E. MARIEN, *Oud-België, van de eerste landbouwers tot de komst van Caesar* (with extensive bibliography), Antwerp, 1952.

Een kwart eeuw oudheidkundig bodemonderzoek in Nederland (Gedenboek A. E. van Giffen), Meppel, 1947.

Algemene Geschiedenis der Nederlanden, vol. I: H. DANTHINE, *De praehistorie van het Zuiden;* A. W. BIJVANCK, *De praehistorie van het Noorden,* Antwerp-Utrecht, 1949.

Works on the Prehistory of Smaller Areas

P. C. J. A. BOELES, *Friesland tot de elfde eeuw,* The Hague, 1951.

A. E. VAN GIFFEN, *Opgravingen in Drente* (in: *Drente, een handboek voor het kennen van het Drentse leven in voorbije eeuwen*), Meppel, 1943.

H. J. and G. A. J. BECKERS, *Voorgeschiedenis van Zuid-Limburg,* Maastricht, 1940.

H. VAN DE WEERD and R. DE MAEYER, *De Oudste Geschiedenis* (in: *De Geschiedenis van Vlaanderen,* vol. I), Antwerp, 1936.

The Low Countries
Studies on Special Subjects

CHAPTERS I & II

H. Breuil and L. Koslowski, *Etudes de stratigraphie paléolithique dans le Nord de la France, la Belgique et l'Angleterre* (in: *L'Anthropologie*, 44, 1934, pp. 249-290).

J. de Heinzelin de Braucourt, *Présentation des gisements paléolithiques de la Belgique dans le cadre des régions naturelles* (*Bull. Institut royal des Sciences Naturelles de Belgique*, vol. XXV, 1949, No. 17).

A. Bohmers, *Jong-Palaeolithicum en Vroeg-Mesolithicum* (in: *Een kwart eeuw oudheidkundig bodemonderzoek in Nederland*, pp. 129-199).

CHAPTER III

J. G. D. Clark, *The Mesolithic Settlement of Northern Europe*, Cambridge, 1936.

H. Schwabedissen, *Die Federmesser-Gruppen des nordwesteuropäischen Flachlandes*, Neumünster, 1954.

CHAPTER IV

J. Hamal-Nandrin, J. Servais and M. Louis, *L'Omalien* (in: *Bull. Soc. d'Anthrop. Brux.*, 51, 1936, pp. 25-125).

W. Buttler, *Der donauländische und der westische Kulturkreis der Jüngeren Steinzeit*, Berlin, 1938.

CHAPTER V

S. Piggott, *The Neolithic Cultures of the British Isles*, Cambridge, 1954.

G. Bailloud and P. Mieg de Boofzheim, *Les civilisations néolithiques de la France dans leur contexte européen*, Paris, 1955.

E. VOGT, *Die Herkunft der Michelsberg Kultur* (in: *Acta Archaeologica* XXIV, 1953, pp. 174 *ff.*).

S. PIGGOTT, *Windmill Hill, East or West?* (in: *Proceedings Preh. Soc.,* XXI, 1955, pp. 96 *ff.*).

P. COLMAN, *Spiennes néolithique* (to be published in: *Bull. Chercheurs de la Wallonnie*).

S. J. DE LAET, *Etudes récentes et documents nouveaux sur la civilisation de Michelsberg* (to be published in: *Bull. Soc. r. belge d'Anthrop. et de Préhistoire,* 1956).

A. E. VAN GIFFEN, *De Hunebedden in Nederland,* 3 vols., Utrecht, 1925.

L. KAELAS, *Wann sind die erste Megalithgräber in Holland entstanden?* (in: *Palaeohistoria,* IV, pp. 47–79).

CHAPTER VI

J. D. VAN DER WAALS and W. GLASBERGEN, *Beaker Types and their Distribution in the Netherlands* (in: *Palaeohistoria,* IV, pp. 5–46).

A. E. VAN GIFFEN, *Die Bauart der Einzelgräber,* 2 vols., Leipzig, 1930.

M. E. MARIEN, *La civilisation des gobelets en Belgique* (in: *Bull. Musées r. d'Art et d'Histoire,* 20, 1948, pp. 16-48).

V. G. CHILDE and N. SANDARS, *La civilisation de Seine-Oise-Marne* (in: *L'Anthropologie,* 54, 1950, pp. 1-18).

M. E. MARIEN, *La civilisation de Seine-Oise-Marne en Belgique* (in: *L'Anthropologie,* 56, 1952, pp. 87-92).

CHAPTER VII

CH. J. COMHAIRE, *Les premiers âges du métal dans les bassins de la Meuse et de l'Escaut* (in: *Bull. Soc. Anthr. Bruxelles,* 13, 1894-1895, pp. 97-226).

M. E. Marien, *Coup d'oeil sur l'étude de l'âge du Bronze en Belgique* (in: *Hand. Maatsch. Gesch. en Oudh. Gent,* N.R.5, 1951, pp. 215 ff.).

S. J. de Laet, *Données nouvelles sur l'âge du Bronze et les débuts de l'âge du Fer en Flandre* (in: *Crónica del IV Congreso Internacional de Ciencias preh. y protoh.,* Madrid, 1954; Zaragoza, 1956, pp. 569 ff.).

W. Glasbergen, *Barrow Excavations in the Eight Beatitudes. The Bronze Age Cemetery between Toterfout and Halve Mijl, North Brabant* (in: *Palaeohistoria,* II, 1954, pp. 1-134; III, 1954, pp. 1-204).

W. Kersten. *Die niederrheinische Grabhügelkultur: zur Vorgeschichte des Niederrheins im 1 Jahrtausend vor Christus* (in: *Bonner Jahrbücher,* 147, 1948, pp. 5-80).

W. J. A. Willems, *Een Bijdrage tot de kennis der Voor-Romeinsche Urnenvelden in Nederland,* Maastricht, 1935.

S. J. de Laet, J. A. E. Nenquin and P. Spitaels, *Contributions à l'étude de la civilisation des Champs d'Urnes en Flandre* (to be published as vol. IV of the *Dissertationes Archaeologicae Gandenses*).

CHAPTERS VIII & IX

C. F. C. Hawkes and G. C. Dunning, *The Belgae of Gaul and Britain* (in: *Archaeolog. Journal,* 87, 1930, pp. 150-335).

V. Tourneur, *Les Belges avant César,* Brussels, 1944.

I am indebted to my colleague H. T. Waterbolk, of the University of Groningen, for the drawings of figures 17 and 18, and to my colleague W. Glasbergen, of the University of Amsterdam, for the drawings of figures 26 (drawing P. C. A. van der Kamp) and 33. Figure 34 is re-produced with the kind permission of my colleague A. E. van Giffen (University of Groningen).

My assistant J. A. E. Nenquin has made the drawings for figures 2–16, 19–25, 27–31 (3, 4 and 5 after Breuil and Koslowski, 8 after Twiessel-mann, 11 and 12 after Bohmers, 13 after Hamal-Nandrin and Ophoven, 14 after Rahir, 15 after Lequeux, Hamal-Nandrin and Servais, 16 after Philippe, 19 and 20 after Hamal-Nandrin, Servais and Louis, 23, 24, 29 and 31 after A. E. van Giffen, 27 after de Loë). The other drawings are original ones, based on material in the Royal Institute of Natural Sciences at Brussels (6, 7, 9, 10, 21), the Royal Museum of Art and History at Brussels (28 and 30), the Butchers' Hall Museum at Antwerp (22), the museum of Sint-Niklaas-Waas (25).

Original photographs for the plates were supplied by the author (41); the Royal Institute of Natural Sciences at Brussels (1, 2, 3, 4); the Royal Museum of Art and History at Brussels (copyright ACL) (5, 6, 9, 11, 12, 13, 34, 35, 43, 51, 52, 53, 54, 56, 60, 61); the State Museum of Antiquities at Leyden (26, 27, 28, 29, 31, 45, 50, 57); the Biological-Archaeological Institute of the University at Groningen (7, 15, 16, 17, 18, 19, 20, 21, 22, 23, 25, 30, 36, 37, 38, 39, 40, 47, 48, 49); the Museum of Mariemont (55, 62); the Butchers' Hall Museum at Antwerp (8); the Curtius Museum at Liège (10); the Archaeological Museum at Assen (24); the Frisian Museum at Leeuwarden (44); the University Museum at Ghent (42, 46); Collection Alastair B. Martin at New York (photos Ch. Uht) (58, 59); the ACL at Brussels (32, 33); M. G. Lefrancq at Mons (14); M. J. Mutsaerts at Namur (63).

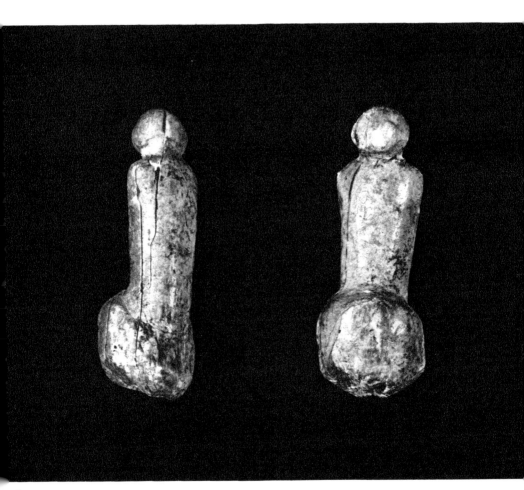

1

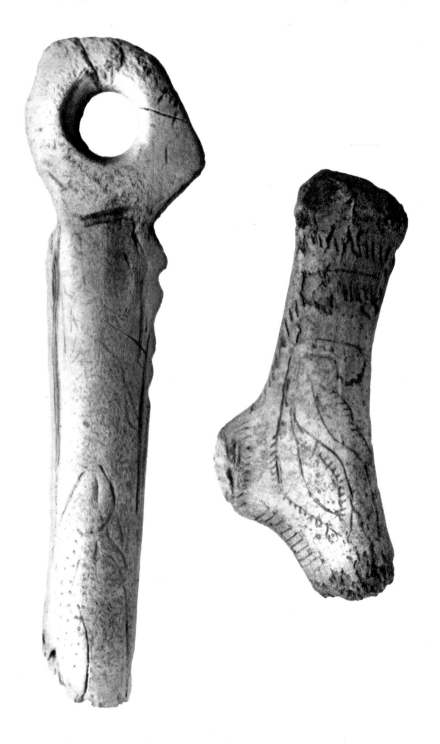

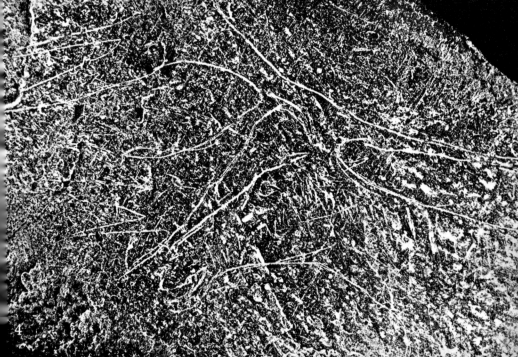

4

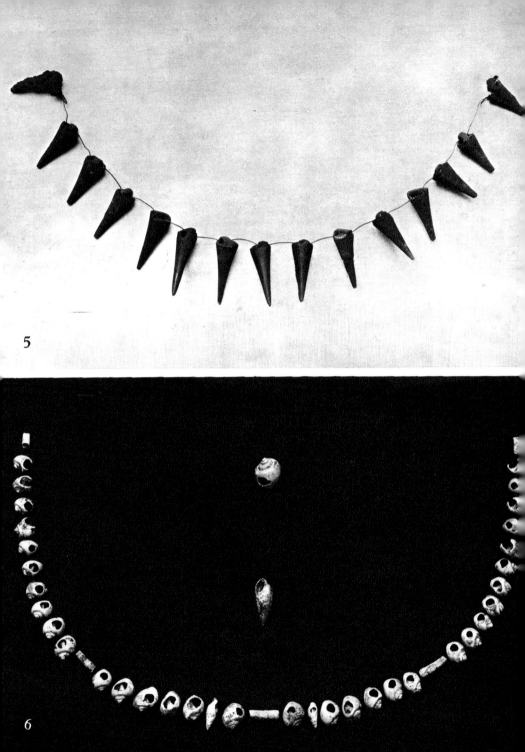

5

6

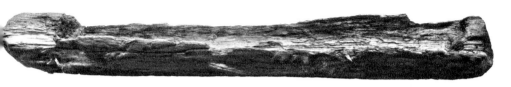

7

8

9

10

11

12

13

14

15

16

18

19

20

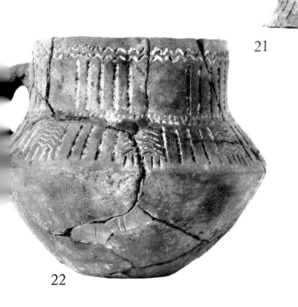

21

22

23

24

26

27

28

29

30

31

32

34

35

36

37

38

39

40

41

42

43

44

45

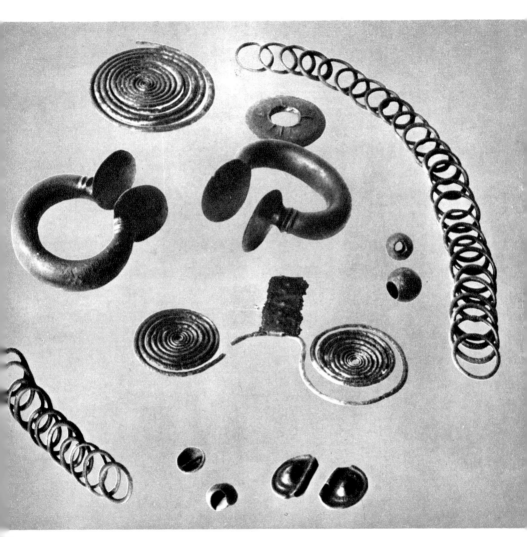

47

48

50

51

52

53

54

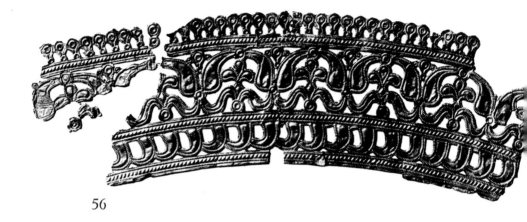

56

57

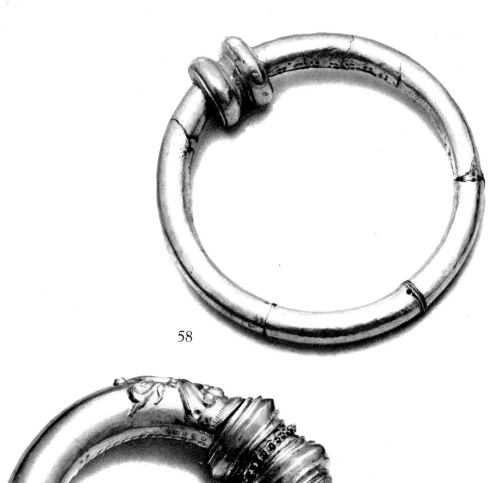

58

59

60

61

63

1 The 'Venus' from the Trou-Magrite at Pont-à-Lesse, a mammoth-ivory figurine. Height: 1⅝ in. (4 cm.). Royal Institute of Natural Sciences, Brussels.

2 (*a*) A *bâton de commandement* found in the third cave at Goyet (prov. Namur) decorated with engraved fishes. Length: 5½ in. (14 cm.).
(*b*) Fragment of reindeer-antler from the Trou-Magrite at Pont-à-Lesse (prov. Namur) engraved with decorative elements. Royal Institute of Natural Sciences, Brussels.

3 *Bos primigenius* and deer engraved on a broken slab of sandstone (psammite) from the Trou de Châleux (prov. Namur). Length: 31½ in. (80 cm.); breadth: 18½ in. (47 cm.). Royal Institute of Natural Sciences, Brussels.

4 Head and neck of a deer engraved on a schist tablet from the Trou de Châleux (prov. Namur). Dimensions: 5⅛ in. × 2½ in. (13·2 cm. × 6·5 cm.). Royal Institute of Natural Sciences, Brussels.

5 Necklace made of a series of small bronze conical hangers, from a grave of the urnfield of Luiksgestel (North Brabant). Royal Museum of Art and History, Brussels.

6 Necklace of perforated shells found in the Remouchamps cave (prov. Liège). Royal Museum of Art and History, Brussels.

7 Mesolithic fire-hollowed canoe, made of a pine trunk. Found near Pesse (Drenthe). Length: almost 10 ft. (3 m.).

8 Four Maglemosean bone points, found at Zele (East Flanders). Length of the second from the left: 7½ in. Others to scale. Butchers' Hall Museum, Antwerp.

9 Three Omalian pots from the Danubian village of Vaux-et-Borset (prov. Liège). Height: 1⅝ in. Royal Museum of Art and History, Brussels.

N

10 Omalian pot from the Danubian village of Omal (prov. Liège). Height: approx. 3 in. Curtius Museum, Liège.

11, 12 Two Omalian pots from the village of Vaux-et-Borset (prov. Liège). Height: $5\frac{1}{2}$ in. Royal Museum of Art and History, Brussels.

13 Michelsberg pottery found at Spiennes (prov. Hainaut). Height of spherical pot: $7\frac{1}{8}$ in. Others to scale. Royal Museum of Art and History, Brussels.

14 Mine gallery at Spiennes, with vertical shaft and disused galleries filled in with chalk blocks (prov. Hainaut).

15 View of the excavations of the 'Eppies bergje' at Odoorn (prov. Drenthe) with grave-pit surrounded by a narrow circular foundation trench, a stone revetment and a deep peripheral ditch.

16 *Hunebed* D.53 at Havelte (prov. Drenthe).

17 Silhouette of a body lying on its side with legs slightly bent, found at Elp, in tumulus II (commune of Westerbolk). All traces of the body have disappeared, but it has left its imprint in the soil in the form of a dark colouring seen clearly against the light sand of the original surface of the soil. Excavated by A. E. van Giffen, 1932.

18–22 Pottery of the Funnel-beaker civilization. Heights: $3\frac{7}{8}$, $8\frac{1}{4}$, $5\frac{1}{2}$, $3\frac{7}{8}$, $6\frac{1}{4}$ in. resp. Biological-Archaeological Institute, Groningen University.

23 Amber beads and copper spirals found in *hunebed* D.28 at Buinen (prov. Drenthe). Left-hand copper spiral 2 in. long. Others to scale.

24 Necklace found in a barrow at Exloo-Odoorn (prov. Drenthe), composed of twenty-five tin beads, fourteen amber beads and four segmented faience beads. Actual size. Arch. Museum, Assen.

25 Timber trackway at Valthe (prov. Drenthe).

26 Large 'pot-beaker' found at Stroeërzand (prov. Guelders). State Museum of Antiquities, Leyden.

27 Veluwe beaker found at the Uddelermeer (prov. Guelders). Height: 7⅝ in. State Museum of Antiquities, Leyden.

28 'Contracted' bell-beaker found at Emmen (prov. Drenthe). Height: 7¾in. State Museum of Antiquities, Leyden.

29 Beaker with protruding foot, found at Renkum (prov. Guelders). Height: 7⅝ in. State Museum of Antiquities, Leyden.

30 Beaker with protruding foot found at Eext (prov. Drenthe). Height: 6⅞ in.

31 Large amphora found at Staverden (prov. Guelders). Height: 11⅝ in. State Museum of Antiquities, Leyden.

32 Gallery-grave at Wéris (prov. Luxembourg).

33 The 'Pierre qui tourne' at Velaine-sur-Sambre (prov. Namur).

34 Gold *lunula* of Irish origin, found at Fauvillers (prov. Luxembourg). Scale: approx. 3:4. Royal Museum of Art and History, Brussels.

35 Gold bracelet dredged from the River Scheldt at Wichelen (prov. East Flanders). Max. internal diam.: 2⅝ in. Royal Museum of Art and History, Brussels.

36 Bronze dagger from Bargeroostervelde (prov. Drenthe), with horn handle decorated with small tin nails. Length: 6 in.

37 Hilversum-urn from barrow 1B of the Toterfout-Halve Mijl cemetery at Veldhoven (prov. North Brabant). Height: 11⅝ in.

38 Excavation of barrow 19 of the Toterfout-Halve Mijl cemetery at Veldhoven (prov. North Brabant).

39, 40 Two Drakenstein-urns from secondary burials in barrow 1B of the Toterfout-Halve Mijl cemetery at Veldhoven (prov. North Brabant). Heights: 13, 12¼ in. resp.

41 Flat grave from the urnfield at Aalter-Oostergem (prov. East Flanders).

42 Late Bronze Age and Early Iron Age pottery from the urnfield at Aalter-Oostergem (prov. East Flanders). Heights of four larger pots, l. to r.: $8\frac{1}{4}$, $7\frac{1}{2}$, $7\frac{1}{8}$, $7\frac{1}{2}$ in. Ghent University Museum.

43 *Kerbschnitt*-bowl from the urnfield at Luiksgestel (prov. North Brabant). Diam.: $7\frac{1}{8}$ in. Royal Museum of Art and History, Brussels.

44 Bronze knife from Appelsga (Frisia). Length: $14\frac{1}{8}$ in. Frisian Museum, Leeuwarden.

45 Ritually bent iron sword with the handle decorated with gold sheet, found in the tomb at Oss (prov. North Brabant). Total length: 2 ft. $11\frac{3}{8}$ in. State Museum of Antiquities, Leyden.

46 Grave goods from the tomb at Port-Arthur (Ghent) (prov. East Flanders). Ext. diam. of two bracelets: $3\frac{7}{8}$ in. Other objects to scale. Ghent University Museum.

47 Excavation of an urnfield at Vledder (prov. Drenthe).

48 Excavation of an urnfield at Wessinghuizen-Onstwedde (prov. Groningen).

49 Excavation of the *terp* at Ezinge. Traces of houses of the oldest period (prov. Frisia).

50 Bronze *situla* found at Baarlo (prov. Dutch Limburg). Height: $16\frac{1}{2}$ in. State Museum of Antiquities, Leyden.

51 Bronze *oenochoe* from Eigenbilzen (Belgian Limburg). Height: $10\frac{1}{2}$ in. Royal Museum of Art and History, Brussels.

52 Bronze bucket from Eigenbilzen (Belgian Limburg). Height: $9\frac{1}{2}$ in. Royal Museum of Art and History, Brussels.

53 Early La Tène carinated pot from Rijkevorsel (prov. Antwerp). Royal Museum of Art and History, Brussels.

54 Early La Tène carinated pot from Gentbrugge (prov. East Flanders.) Height: 4¾ in. Royal Museum of Art and History, Brussels.

55 Fire-dog of 'le Chauffour' at Chapelle-lez-Herlaimont (prov. Hainaut). Height: 9½ in. Museum of Mariemont.

56 Gold ornamental band from Eigenbilzen (Belgian Limburg). Width: 2⅜ in. Royal Museum of Art and History, Brussels.

57 Silver disc from Helden (prov. Dutch Limburg). Diam.: 8⅝ in. State Museum of Antiquities, Leyden.

58 Smaller gold torque from Frasnes-lez-Buissenal (prov. Hainaut). Diam.: 4¾ in. Collection Alastair B. Martin, New York.

59 Larger gold torque from Frasnes-lez-Buissenal (prov. Hainaut). Diam.: approx. 8 in. Collection Alastair B. Martin, New York.

60 Early La Tène pottery from La Panne (prov. West Flanders). Height: 7⅛ in. Royal Museum of Art and History, Brussels.

61 Late La Tène pottery from La Panne (prov. West Flanders). Height: 7 in. Royal Museum of Art and History, Brussels.

62 Grave goods from tomb I at Ciply (prov. Hainaut). Museum of Mariemont. Scale: approx. 1:4.

63 The *oppidum* at Hastedon, Saint-Servais (prov. Namur). Total area: 32 acres.

Index